Genealogical Standards of Evidence

GENEALOGIST'S REFERENCE SHELF

Genealogical Standards of Evidence

A Guide for Family Historians

BRENDA DOUGALL MERRIMAN

DUNDURN PRESS
TORONTO

Editor: Ruth Chernia   Proofreader: Allison Hirst
Design: Courtney Horner   Printer: Transcontinental

Library and Archives Canada Cataloguing in Publication

Merriman, Brenda Dougall
Genealogical standards of evidence : a guide for family historians / by Brenda Dougall Merriman.

(Genealogist's reference shelf)
Previously published under title: About genealogical standards of evidence.
Includes bibliographical references.
ISBN 978-1-55488-451-3

1. Genealogy. I. Ontario Genealogical Society II. Merriman, Brenda Dougall. About genealogical standards of evidence. III. Title. IV. Series: Genealogist's reference shelf

CS88.A1M47 2010   929'.1072   C2009-907197-5

1 2 3 4 5   14 13 12 11 10

We acknowledge the support of the **Canada Council for the Arts** and the **Ontario Arts Council** for our publishing program. We also acknowledge the financial support of the **Government of Canada** through the **Book Publishing Industry Development Program** and **The Association for the Export of Canadian Books**, and the **Government of Ontario** through the **Ontario Book Publishers Tax Credit program**, and the **Ontario Media Development Corporation**.

Care has been taken to trace the ownership of copyright material used in this book. The author and the publisher welcome any information enabling them to rectify any references or credits in subsequent editions.

J. Kirk Howard, President

Printed and bound in Canada.
www.dundurn.com

Ontario Genealogical Society
Suite 102, 40 Orchard View Boulevard
Toronto, Ontario, Canada M4R 1B9
tel. (416) 489-0734   fax. (416) 489-9803
provoffice@ogs.on.ca   www.ogs.on.ca

Dundurn Press   Gazelle Book Services Limited   Dundurn Press
3 Church Street, Suite 500   White Cross Mills   2250 Military Road
Toronto, Ontario, Canada   High Town, Lancaster, England   Tonawanda, NY
M5E 1M2   LA1 4XS   U.S.A. 14150

CONTENTS

ACKNOWLEDGEMENTS

It was my privilege to serve for six years as a trustee on the Board for Certification of Genealogists, during the great period when genealogical principles and standards were being defined on their own terms. In the twenty-first century, genealogy and family history will reach greater heights of recognition and acceptance as an independent field of historical study.

My thanks go to the colleagues who originally encouraged me to develop this manuscript, and to my associates who kindly reviewed it. Special acknowledgement goes to Alison Hare, CG, for being there. Any deviations and errors are solely mine.

INTRODUCTION

Q: Why read this book?

A: It is intended as an introduction to the habits of careful researchers; an inexpensive reference work for checking the research notes you compile; and as a supplement to courses, workshops, or seminars you may have attended.

- This book will explain how the genealogical community developed standards of evidence and documentation, what those basic standards are, and how you can apply them to your own work.

- This book will *not* tell you how to find the sources you need for your own research or how to trace your ancestors in detail. You can learn more about family history sources and research techniques from many expertly written manuals and the courses and conferences offered by genealogical societies.

One of the greatest attractions of genealogy and family history is that each of us has a unique nuclear family, shared only by our birth siblings. Thus, discovering our family history begins as an absorbing personal pastime to find the parents of our parents and so on. Soon, however, it will begin to overlap with cousins and descendants of earlier generations as we meet them. Some of them will be researchers, too. Genealogists also frequently share such common connections as ethnic origins or migration patterns. Few other hobbies or professions provide such enjoyment in the hunt, the thrill of discovery, the satisfaction of solving problems.

You might ask, what is the difference between a genealogist and a family historian? Essentially, they have become the same (the terms are used interchangeably in this book). In the past, genealogists tended to compile rather dry tomes of multi-generational names and vital statistics; family historians often produced a labour of love with little reference to solid sources of information. Traditionally, the genealogist followed more or less acceptable formats and a family historian used a more fluid style of presentation. Now most of us aim for the same goal: a well-documented narrative that tells the story of ancestors, not merely a "tree" with bare names and dates. *Family tree* seems to be a rather generic term these days for almost any family history project, whereas more properly it refers to a chart or diagram of names and relationships.

Genealogical evidence is the information — evaluated and analyzed — that allows us to *identify* an individual, an event in his or her life, or the relationship between individuals. Genealogy and family history revolve around issues of identification. In describing how we establish or argue an identification, we use such words as *evidence* or *proof* or *source documentation*.

By its very nature, the construction of a genealogy requires evidence or proof for the linking of generations. If your cousin insists that your family is descended from William the Conqueror or Louis Riel or the *Mayflower* passengers, what does he use to substantiate this claim? His grandmother told him, so it must be true (Grandma was the soul of honesty)? He saw it in a book (title and author long forgotten)? He picked it up from that website with the smileys on it? With computers now a fairly staple household fixture, the Internet brings us its dazzling assortment of information. We don't necessarily discount the value of family hearsay or the convenience of compiled databases, but they don't replace tried-and-true methodology for documenting each step of good research.

Later in this book, you will see examples of sources that illustrate some of the research issues to watch for and evaluate. For instance, deaths often produce a wider sampling of record sources than any other major event in the family cycle. There may be variations in the information they contain about one individual. A family history is not complete without a discussion of such anomalies, requiring analytic skills.

Sharing, Preserving, Networking

When we first get caught up in this addictive hobby, few of us realize how much material we will collect and what we will do with it. Some of us acquire filing cabinets or cardboard cartons full of notes and copies of documents. We collect taped interviews with family members or precious, ancient photographs and heirlooms. Along the way, the discovery of new cousins is not an uncommon occurrence. We may have begun our quest merely to satisfy our own curiosity, but become dedicated detectives in the search for family truths.

Most of us reach a stage where we feel an obligation (or unrestrained enthusiasm!) to share our latest information with family members. At the very least, we have new details to relate at the next family reunion. But, don't forget, there is always a much wider interest, perhaps among the local genealogical society we joined or in the community from which the ancestors originated. The information we uncover may strike a responsive chord in another researcher with a similar ethnic background, or with the same religious heritage or geographic interest. Libraries with genealogy collections and societies with libraries welcome family histories in many forms.

Whatever we learn about our own family has interest for someone else — somewhere — maybe a grandchild or a niece, a stranger in a distant society or country, maybe newfound relatives from a "missing" or collateral line. What begins as a very personal study of genealogy grows to emphasize our kinship with genealogists and family historians across borders and through time. Although we work in the past, we know the future holds descendants willing to carry on and supplement the infinite progression.

We should realize the intrinsic value of our labours, over months and years of research, is surely worth preserving for posterity. And that labour is worth preserving in a form that strives to meet quality standards as well as engaging our family readers.

There are many tangible forms for preserving and sharing our work. Normally we record information as our research progresses. Some of us work with pencilled charts and family file folders. Some of us use genealogical software as a database for all the individual ancestors. Eventually we must make some decisions for making our work results more accessible and ensuring it survives us — decisions about an end goal, about producing a family history or choosing smaller, more manageable intermediate goals. A variety of presentations gives us options to choose an aspect that best suits our skills and timing (more in chapter 3, Learning and Practice).

The good news is that help is always out there for all of us, at any stage of the process. Since you are reading this book, you will have become aware of, or are already plugged into the available support systems. Sadly, we do not always reach the isolated family historian, the self-taught genealogist who works in a vacuum, reinventing the wheel, blissfully unaware of a great international network. Splendid solitude may enhance the work of a creative *artiste*, but a family historian needs solid empirical skills and ongoing contact with new developments. We should all be encouraging such people to join with us.

The bottom line is to understand and collate the information we get, wherever it comes from. While our gathered information is due (ideally) to our own research efforts, we also receive information from our relatives, from reciprocal exchanges with distant researchers, or from hired professional genealogists. Information received from others usually needs backtracking to an original source. Ultimately we must analyze its evidentiary value before making judgments about identifications and relationships.

The standards of evidence discussed in this booklet are twenty-first-century mainstream. It takes time for mainstream awareness to reach individuals, and even societies, who lack contact with the large or national organizations that lead our thriving community.

Leaders in the field of genealogy have worked long and hard, and continue to work, to demonstrate that family history is no longer a poor sister to allied scholarly fields. Demographers, historians of all persuasions, social anthropologists, genetic counsellors, probate courts, estate lawyers, and many others are seeing the results from adhering to standards of excellence in genealogy. It is up to each and all of us as responsible genealogists — whether we work at family history as a pleasant pastime, as part-time volunteers for our societies, or as paid researchers — to do our best to reach for and apply those standards.

CHAPTER I

The Background

Q: Why do I need to know any background about the study of genealogy?

A: To increase your awareness of the larger community you participate in; to promote scholarship and fellowship while being aware of unethical activities; to support your own growing expertise among potential skeptics.

A brief overview of the past and the present will make us aware of the need to recognize competence and avoid dishonest practices. The popular pursuit of ancestors as we know it today was not always enjoyed by people like you and me. In times past, it was an exercise of the aristocracy, heralds, and landed gentry — the only beneficiaries of such a study. Heraldic authorities have existed since medieval times to record the progeny of leading families for matters of legal inheritance. Titles, land, fortunes, even kingdoms were not the only substantial benefits of proven succession. In the British Isles and Europe, the length of your pedigree or your heritable expectations have been a distinct social asset regardless of financial circumstances.

As in other disciplines that strive for standards of excellence, there are the few who blight the credibility of genuine genealogical research. Some examples result from careless or inadequate research. Others are deliberate frauds. The occasional fabrication of "impeccable" lineages for residual gain was a temptation that began long ago. Anthony Camp, former director of the Society of Genealogists in London, documented some historical occurrences in Britain, in his article "Forgery and Deception in Genealogy."[1] Falsifying documents is not a new phenomenon. Such things happen here and there, even in modern times. Unscrupulous people can take advantage of the unwary or the pompous by inventing what they want to see, expecting that their work will not be examined. Auspiciously, our present world of fast communications alerts us to dubious enterprises and discourages unethical behaviour.

Leading genealogists are exposing dishonest claims and lineages, whether intentional or inadvertent. Although the plagiarism of Alex Haley (*Roots*) was exposed in a civil lawsuit, just as important was the refutation of his claims to precise African origins and ancestral timing by the meticulous research of Gary B. Mills and Elizabeth Shown Mills.[2] More recently, Boston-area genealogist Sharon Sergeant and others were instrumental in documenting the literary hoax *Misha: A Memoir of the Holocaust Years*. Forensic genealogy and the demonstration of genealogical standards more than hold their own in courts of law.

On a different angle, enthusiastic businesses still sell "family histories" marketed to the unsuspecting who want instant gratification. They are sold as *The [insert your Surname here] Family History* or similar titles, often packaged with a colourful heraldic cover. Besides a summary of the surname origin and locations where it occurs, the most relevant part is perhaps only a random list of telephone directory entries. Dr. Helen Hinchliff of British Columbia once chaired the Ethics Committee of the National Genealogical Society to produce a 120-page report on the dubious activities of mail-order firms.[3] Such companies, whose names change regularly, are simply scam operators who prey on a gullible market. They would have us believe that everyone with the same surname is just one big family. More recently, the Internet has opened up the potential for websites of unreliable products. Mass-produced items make no attempt to connect to *you*, where your family history begins.

Equally unacceptable are heraldic devices purveyed as "family coats of arms." Again, the ignorant are led to believe that armigerous bearings (which are legal property granted to one person) can be appropriated by anyone of the same surname. Sad to say, even the field of practising professional genealogists has seen the occasional invasion of phony credentials. "Certificates" with postnominal initials have been offered for nothing more than a goodly sum of money.

I won't dwell longer on a small, shadowy area of genealogy, because it's not difficult now to verify the quality of credentials or products. It takes more effort to properly examine and understand each source we use ourselves. This is why we need to stay informed, keep up with news, learn to network. The field of genealogy has reached a new assertive era with eminent advocates and educators. Ours is but to emulate!

North America

On this side of the Atlantic, the study of genealogy has shed the old stigma of elitism faster than in European cultures. The old notion of pedigrees "for gain or brag" still exists among some who dismiss genealogy, but has been greatly overwhelmed due to the huge popular interest of the last few generations.

Genealogical study has been active in North America since at least the nineteenth century. Our earliest French, English,

Dutch, and Spanish settlers, who left centuries of legacy, differed in their political and religious backgrounds and their motives for emigrating. Many more ethnic and cultural groups have since joined the remarkable heritage mix on this continent. The once historical pattern of British emigration through ports like Quebec, New York, and Philadelphia, and our major North American migration pattern of east to west, lead thousands of genealogists back to these eastern areas, at some point, to search for their emigrant ancestors. From there, we all want to connect to "the old country." And, more recently, descendents of the aboriginal inhabitants of North America have joined the quest in seeking to establish their lineages.

Hundreds of genealogical publications began appearing in the late nineteenth and early twentieth centuries. Some were well-researched and well-documented, inasmuch as the times and access to sources allowed. Some depended heavily on the oral or written recollections of descendants, well after the described events occurred — accounting for some deficiency in reference citations for the genealogical statements being made. In fact, many of the records we are now able to consult were simply not accessible when many of these books were published. We are very fortunate today that so much work is ongoing to recover lost documentary material, to restore and catalogue it, and to prepare finding aids and indexes.

Consulting publications of founding families and ancient pedigrees should never be understood as *proof* of anything. The next chapter will discuss trusting the printed or published word.

In the twentieth century, more and more genealogical societies were formed to provide support, information, and fellowship for growing numbers of family historians. Societies began publishing their own periodicals to assist their membership and preserve local information. Workshops and other methods of instruction became necessary. Textbooks began to proliferate. The custodians of the source materials used by genealogists — archivists, librarians, and government officials — have had to recognize and adapt to this surge in public demand. Natural leaders in the field emerged as teachers and authors of educational materials, and advocates for the preservation of and access to historical documents. Journals were publishing updates and corrections to the older "classic" publications.

Another adjunct to the interest in family history and pedigrees was the development of specialized societies. A few examples of lineage societies are: Daughters of the American Revolution, Descendants of Charlemagne, the Mayflower Society, and the United Empire Loyalists' Association of Canada. Membership is predicated upon your ability to show evidence of direct descent from a certain qualified ancestor. Some societies have been taken to the nth degree, even to the organizing of illegitimate descendants of specific monarchs or black sheep ancestors. An arguably comparable concept is the more flexible approach of "one-name" or surname societies and the eclectic Scottish clan associations.

Methodology

One of the landmarks in the study of genealogy on this continent was the appearance in 1930 of a book called *Genealogy as Pastime and Profession* by Donald Lines Jacobus, a man considered by his peers and honoured today as "the founder of this modern American school of critical genealogists."[4] At that time there may have been thousands of family histories in print, but there was scarcely one about the techniques and methods of sound genealogical research. It is a fitting tribute to this man's talent and perception, that almost eighty years later the book is still relevant

— and even compelling — reading. As a sidebar, Jacobus's legacy continues in the prestigious periodical he also founded, now called *The American Genealogist.*

As interest in family history grew, genealogists began to recognize the parallels between their own work and the legal preparation for court cases. Family detective work — its gathering of evidence and arguing of proof — seemed to suit the precedents of the legal tradition. Established phrases were borrowed from this field, such as the *preponderance of evidence* principle, to be discussed in the next chapter. Genealogist, attorney, and author Noel Stevenson was an instrumental leader in clearly describing those advances in methodological practice.

In the twenty-first century, the study of genealogy surged beyond this borrowing phase. For some time, respected genealogy journals had been requiring certain scholarly standards in their submissions. In effect, this meant publishing articles with carefully weighed case studies of identity and relationships, with well-cited sources. The Board for Certification of Genealogists published its landmark *The BCG Genealogical Standards Manual* to give cohesion and clarified form to the principles in consensual usage.

Ultimately, serious genealogical research exhibits a higher degree of demonstrated evidence than traditional academic history or even most legal standards.

Resources and Access

Meanwhile, relevant materials and sources of information were becoming easier to access. Before the availability of the Internet at the end of the twentieth century, researching ancestors in a distant area was a slow process. So often the answers to questions and contact with others were dependent on postal mail.

The Church of Jesus Christ of Latter-day Saints (popularly called Mormons) created the world-renowned Family History Library (FHL) in Salt Lake City, the repository for microfilm copies of millions of genealogical records from around the globe. Access to the FHL and to information and databases on its *FamilySearch* website is free. The FHL has Family History Centers in many countries where its microfilms can be borrowed. Their online catalogue facilitates preparation for ordering films or a research visit to Utah.

Similarly, government-affiliated repositories play an important role as custodians of source material relevant to genealogy. The National Archives and Records Administration (NARA) in Washington, D.C., and Library and Archives Canada in Ottawa are constantly working to place online more descriptions of their massive collections of original documents and finding aids. Many useful microfilmed sources can be borrowed through public library systems. Digital images of their resources are coming online, sometimes in partnership with commercial concerns. Digitized historical books are now more common online with the cooperation of libraries and other resource centres.

Other public and private libraries also maintain major genealogy collections worth extended visits. A few in the United States are: the Allen County Public Library in Fort Wayne, Indiana; the Newberry Library in Chicago; the Daughters of the American Revolution Library in Washington, D.C.; and the Boston Public Library. Large genealogy societies have also made their library catalogues available online. Most are freely searchable but with hands-on access for members only. Societies are adapting to the Internet world by offering such online membership benefits. Researchers have information at their fingertips that only a few years ago would have taken much longer to find.

Personal websites and commercial services for genealogical consumption developed quickly along with the Internet — a phenomenon growing everywhere on the globe. *Ancestry.com* is a popular subscription-based service, although *Footnote.com* and *WorldVitalRecords.com* are just two others of the many currently online, providing searchable databases either free or by fee. Bear in mind that company and website names have been changing regularly in only the first few years of the twenty-first century because of corporate restructuring and mergers; doubtless more will occur as competition increases. *Rootsweb.com* was one of the earliest Internet presences and continues to host a multitude of mailing lists and message boards. *Ancestry*, *Rootsweb*, and *Genealogy.com* are among many sites and services that became part of The Generations Network corporation — most recently the corporate name reverted to Ancestry.com, the name of its flagship product.

Not to be overlooked is the online *WorldGenWeb*, developed as a network of country and regional volunteers who provide information about local resources.

Skillbuilding

Education for the ever-increasing numbers of novice genealogists became a demanding new reality, especially with the Internet's new brand of curious beginner, who might appropriate derivative material on websites and databases as gospel truth without searching for or seeing original sources.

Beginners are often introduced to genealogy by filling out a chart with their known family names and dates. Discerning instructors are realizing that, even before this step, beginners need an understanding of how to evaluate and analyze the documents that produce those names and dates. Before attempting to fill out that chart, it's better to know all about what *evidence* you are citing for each person's data. Learning evaluation and analysis is most effective when discussing sources such as birth, marriage, and death records of family members personally known by the novice.

Skill is involved along every step of the family history path. Some of us may have an intuitive grasp of the investigative process, while others may need to work a little harder at it. Nevertheless, we all need support and confidence to attain a satisfactory level of competence. Attending conferences, seminars, workshops, and courses has already been mentioned as essential for self-growth. Now there is even more access to learning, from online articles to podcasts and videocasts.

And there are top-level opportunities for validating personal skills. From the American Society of Genealogists came the independent Board for Certification of Genealogists; from the Church of Jesus Christ of Latter-day Saints came their Accreditation Department, now the independent International Commission for the Accreditation of Professional Genealogists. While these bodies evaluate individuals who intend to pursue the professional, business side of genealogy, testing is not limited to "genealogists for hire." Far from it. For example, the BCG encourages all serious family historians to challenge themselves and improve their skill levels and thus uphold the standards of the field as a whole.

The Genealogical Institute of the Maritimes, created in 1983, was a similar leader in Canada. The Bureau québécois d'attestation de compétence en généalogie, based in the city of Quebec, and the Saskatchewan Genealogical Society have also developed programs for their geographic areas. Testing organizations are listed in chapter 3, Learning and Practice.

All these opportunities address the growing desire to discover our personal historical roots — a desire that needs the accompanying awareness of sound research habits and skills. The application of widely acceptable principles in genealogical research and writing benefits all of us alike. Each of us has a family history that deserves the best effort we can put into it.

CHAPTER 2

Genealogical Research Standards

Q: Do I need to know about standards for my own researching? Will standards affect *my* family history?

A: Understanding the standards will help you meet your family history goals at an acknowledged level of competence. If you want to leave a legacy of substance when your days are done — a family history or a report or an article or notes that will endure — striving for standards ensures self-satisfaction as well as peer respect.

A large part of family history research and the genealogical process is identification. The elements of identification are the combination of a name with an exact point in time and a location: name, date, place. We work to apply those elements to the major vital events in an ancestor's life: birth, marriage, death (often abbreviated to BMD). These events form the bare structural outline of an ancestor's life story. Sometimes we describe this beginning as the skeleton of an ancestor to which we want to add flesh, muscle, and even human attributes.

We work backwards in time from the starting point of what we know about ourselves and our parents. Besides determining name-date-place for each ancestor, we must also connect one generation to the next by solid evidence of a relationship. For instance, how do you know your maternal great-grandfather's name? Do you have credible information that states his relationship to his daughter, your grandmother? Is hearing the information from your uncle as reliable as seeing grandma's birth certificate? What other sources could add more information? One source, one bit of information, one piece of evidence is never enough to be satisfactory.

Each step with an ancestor begins with learning his or her name. You are going to build the collection of "identifiers" that distinguish this individual, aiming to establish his or her unique progress through life and death. Each time the name appears in a source, we look for identifiers like age, location, parents, spouse, child, occupation, signature, and so on. Such elements help us link the name to appearances in more records. The position of that ancestor on our family chart, in family files or genealogical software is backed up with thoughtful research planning and careful references.

As you progress, you will be forming hypotheses and/or posing questions to yourself. The hypotheses and questions will shift and re-form on the same point. As a simple case example, we will follow a single thread. For example, *Robert Kent was born about 1873* is a hypothesis. For research purposes, that point can also be re-framed as a question: *What is Robert Kent's date of birth?* Both approaches should lead to thinking about which sources could reveal the necessary information. What kind of sources would be relevant? Is there a birth record for Robert Kent?

This book is intended as a primer and does not attempt to address more complex issues. Suggestions for further, in-depth exploration are in the Reading and Reference section. Genealogical terminology has evolved beyond the academic classifications that label sources as primary and secondary. The terminology is more precise in meaning and relevance for our specific usage. Case studies in genealogy journals illustrate ancestor identification and frequently offer new strategies for developing your own.

The model below is based upon those developed and published by leading board-certified genealogists and should assist you with the discussion that follows. For an inexpensive, concise guide, look for Mills's laminated one-sheet *Evidence Analysis: A Research Process Map.* Another version or "visualization" of the research process and GPS can be seen at Mark Tucker's website: *www.thinkgenealogy.com/wp-content/uploads/Genealogy%20 Research%20Map%20v2.pdf.*

Reference Model

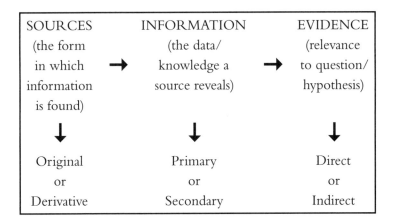

SOURCES	INFORMATION	EVIDENCE
(the form in which information is found)	(the data/ knowledge a source reveals)	(relevance to question/ hypothesis)
Original or Derivative	Primary or Secondary	Direct or Indirect

Sources

Sources provide us with information; they are the physical *form* in which, and from which, we obtain information. Sources can be documents, audio or visual recordings, artifacts, books, people, or Internet sites. Classifying a source involves distinguishing between first and subsequent recordings.

An **original** source is *the first recording of an event,* not derived from an earlier or prior statement of record. It exists in the form in which it was created. Photocopies, photographs, and digital images of original sources are generally treated as being equal to originals, if we are confident that they have not been altered. Customarily we assign more value to an original source.

But original sources are not always available or accessible when we search for them. A government record of birth may not exist because the parents failed to comply with local government requirements. The church register where a marriage was recorded may have been lost in a fire. Cemetery stones become illegible through natural weathering. Many governments withhold access to vital records because of personal data protection (commonly called privacy) legislation.

Our research also broadens to **derivative** sources. These are sources that derive from previously recorded material. Derivative sources are rearranged or transcribed forms, including abstracts and extracts, indexes, compilations, and many publications (print or Internet). Each time a record is copied or repeated, the risk of error is present. We should always be aware of what kind of source we are viewing. Is this an original record, or is it a transcription, a memorial abstract, or a copybook entry? Although well-researched family histories and genealogical compilations are based on research in many original sources (with foot- or endnotes to cite those sources), the works themselves are the author's or compiler's derivations.

> **Case:** If Robert Kent's birth was registered by his father in a timely way in the province of New Brunswick, according to contemporary government requirements, this would be the

earliest and first record of the birth — an **original** source. However, if Robert's birth was found in a series of society articles listing baptisms at a specific church, or if a published family history reveals the same, the articles and the compiler/author's work are **derivative** sources. Tempting as it may be to take them at face value, the diligent researcher perseveres to locate the original sources on which these were based.

You will find a checklist of potentially useful research sources, of both types, following this chapter. The search for sources that could reveal information about each aspect of an ancestor's life should not stop at two or three items that support your hypothesis or seem to answer your question. It is *reasonable* to seek and probe extensive sources that could yield any ancestral information.

Information

We should also distinguish between a source and the information it contains. Quite often a source will contain several pieces of information or data. Information from any source requires examination and evaluation. We refer to **primary** and **secondary** information to denote the degree of quality or credibility.

Primary information is stated by someone with firsthand knowledge of an event, or who witnessed an event. We tend to place more credibility on primary information. An example is the medical attendant or spouse who was present at a death and then registered the information. There is little doubt that the informant knew the name of the deceased and the date and place of death. But many death records contain additional information.

Secondary information is provided by someone with secondhand knowledge of a particular event. The same informant for the death registration may have been required to provide the decedent's date and place of birth, and the names of his or her parents. In many cases, this is not likely to be information of which the informant had firsthand knowledge. A doctor or priest who ministered to a dying adult was probably not present at the time and place of birth. The same informant, even a close relative, may have had only secondhand knowledge of the deceased's birth.

Often-told family stories and hearsay that are passed down through generations are another example of secondary information because the information undergoes "filtering." As the stories are repeated, details can become embroidered or lost. Confusing the identity or relationship of the subject is not uncommon.

Personal letters and diaries are original sources that contain a mixture of information, according to the timeliness of the events they are describing. We also understand that such information can reflect a certain bias on the part of the source, requiring us to weigh each piece in context.

> **Case:** If Robert Kent's father, James, was the person who registered his birth, the information is **primary** because the parent himself was presumably present or nearby when the event was occurring. If Robert Kent's date of birth is given on his death certificate or in a newspaper obituary, the information could be **secondary** because his spouse, child, or a third party — whoever supplied the data — likely only had secondhand knowledge about his birth. But who is the informant for a death certificate or newspaper notices? Can we determine that? If a

parent or older sibling was the informant, he or she could have had primary knowledge. Therefore, categorizing information into primary and secondary is part of our evaluation process to examine the strengths or weaknesses of the information we find.

Evidence

From information we analyze, interpret, and correlate our evidence, i.e., the information relevant to our research question. Evidence is **direct** when it answers our question or hypothesis unequivocally. It is **indirect** when it does not explicitly state the identity, relationship, or event we are trying to establish. With a reasonably exhaustive research, whether we find primary information, direct evidence, or conflicting results, we should be able to offer a convincing case regarding an identity, relationship, or event.

> **Case:** Evidence is **direct** about Robert Kent's date of birth on the timely birth registration. Evidence is **indirect** about his *exact* date of birth when you see Robert as a young child in the 1881 household of James and Charlotte Kent (but direct evidence of his *age*). The birth registration directly answers the question of a precise date. The 1881 census merely asks for ages of the household members. Robert's age given as eight years old implies a calculated year of birth as 1873. This piece of evidence is indirect regarding birth *date*, but may be supportive when combined with more evidence.

Carefully correlated and analyzed indirect evidence may weigh as strongly as any direct evidence. Even direct evidence must be examined with due attention to its source and in correlation to other evidence of independent origin.

Analysis of Evidence

Each piece of information about an ancestor should be examined in the context of its source and analyzed as evidence in conjunction with all the information you collect. The analytic process is not merely asking, "Does this source give information that answers my question or supports my hypothesis?" but also "How qualified is this source to answer my question?" and "How credible is this information?" In other words, who created the source? When, and for what purpose? Was it created under legal oath or in a church sacrament? Who was the informant? Did the creator or informant have any self-interested bias regarding the information? We can't always answer these questions, but we must consider them.

To point out the need for careful examination, both original and derivative sources can harbour misinformation. Just because a source *is* original does not necessarily make it accurate. And at times, primary information can be unintentionally or deliberately erroneous, thus affecting the evidence. This is why family historians and genealogists are urged to hunt down as many relevant sources as are reasonably accessible. The collected evidence may or may not agree with the original hypothesis. Sometimes our hypothesis is not supported by the evidence and then it's time to re-evaluate, forming a new hypothesis.

Case: You may be lucky to find that Robert Kent's father registered his birth as 16 May 1872 with the province of New Brunswick, exactly where you expected it to be. This is primary information from what appears to be an original source that directly answered your question: When was Robert born? Is this enough to make a convincing conclusion? On judging the source itself, how "original" is it? Is it a direct photocopy or printout of the provincial registration? Or is it a typed extract? Or did you find it in a compiled, online database? Regarding the information, did Robert's father register the birth within days, or weeks (or months) of the event? Is the date clearly written? Perhaps at this stage your only other piece of evidence is Robert's age in the 1881 census (eight years old). If you look up the official census date (4 April 1881), you will find Robert could have turned nine years old any day after that during 1881. The census information coincides with a birth in 1872 because Robert would not have turned nine years old until a few weeks after the census was enumerated.

However, the birth registration may not have been the first source you obtained. A birth registration may not even exist. As a diligent researcher, you have been studying other sources for information about the life and death of Robert Kent. Some of that information will have relevance to his date or year of birth. A few examples for our fictitious case demonstrate some preliminary analysis of selected evidence.

- Let's say Robert Kent's baptism was entered in a New Brunswick parish register on 16 June 1872, with his date of birth given as 16 May 1872. Was the original parish register available for viewing and was the script legible? Is the birth information equally reliable as the baptismal date? Are the clergyman's entries in the appropriate sequence? Does the register have extra slips of paper with baptisms of scattered dates? If so, does this indicate some negligence or belated recording by the incumbent? In other words, could an error have crept in? Check the register as a whole for hints to orderly arrangement and chronology.

- Say Robert Kent enlisted in 1914 for First World War service, stating his age as 34 without a corresponding date of birth. The evidence of age is relevant to his year of birth when evidence of an exact date of birth is lacking, because an approximate year can be calculated from his age and the date of the document. Was there a cut-off age for enlisting in the army at that time? It was not uncommon for men to change their age or date of birth to be eligible for military service. Does the information agree with other evidence? A birth year of approximately 1880 may be out of line with other data when you begin to correlate all evidence. "Age" can be weak evidence in circumstances where plausible reasons exist for a person to alter information.

- Another scenario might be Robert's marriage record where his age was requested. Again, because he provided this information about himself, you would probably consider it primary on its own merit as a sole piece of information. You may only get closer to the truth by examining this statement of age in correlation with more evidence. The genealogical sleuth asks, did Robert have any reason to alter his age, for instance to appear more youthful for a much younger bride? Or was he merely, perhaps consistently, careless about stating his age?

- Maybe a distant cousin sent a photocopy of the "births" page from a Kent family Bible. Robert Kent is there with the date 16 June 1872. Can you tell if the Bible was published before or after Robert's year of birth? Can you answer whether the person entering the information was a firsthand, reliable informant? Does this date of birth agree with other evidence? Were the birth entries all written in one hand, as if they were entered at one sitting — thus indicating they were not entered contemporaneously — and many could be subject to memory flaws. Is it possible that the dates of birth and baptism became confused in this source?

The information and evidence we collect, and their sources of origin, require critical attention that leads to deductive reasoning. We examine each source in its context, to evaluate information data for all issues that might have affected credibility, and we analyze the evidence items for the weight of their credibility as applied to our hypothesis or question. Most importantly, all evidence items must be considered together for a logical, sound conclusion about the assertion we want to make. In other words, a conclusion is the summation of well-reasoned analysis after wide-ranging research and evaluation of sources and information. A conclusion relates our process in arriving at any vital and important assertion about the ancestor. Summarizing our evidence in writing is an excellent disciplinary exercise to show how we reached that conclusion. Writing it down is especially necessary when all the evidence is indirect, or contradictory. Then, constructing a proof *argument* is essential to clarify our reasoning. Family research involves this critical evaluation and analysis process many times over.

In our Robert Kent case example, let us say that a civil birth registration does not exist. You have collected:

√ data from the 1881 census with eight-year-old Robert in James and Charlotte Kent's household;

√ information of both his baptism (16 June 1872) and birth (16 May 1872) by viewing the original parish register;

√ a newspaper announcement on 18 May 1872 that Mrs. James Kent gave birth to a son;

√ Robert's death certificate whereon his age indicates a birth year of 1872; and

√ a photocopy of the family Bible page for births with Robert's date as 16 June 1872.

This is building a case — supporting the adjusted hypothesis that Robert was probably born in 1872. You have a sampling of sources with different types of information. Is this enough evidence to draw a convincing conclusion about Robert's exact date of birth? All sources thus far agree on the year. Two sources provide answers to the question of when precisely he was born. But those two pieces of evidence do not agree and will need resolution.

> **Case**: You assert this conclusive statement: Robert Kent was born 16 May 1872. You would elucidate the details and your reasoning by citing the parish register, the newspaper birth notice (which lacks the name of the son) coinciding with a May date, the 1881 census household of James and Charlotte Kent, Robert's death certificate, *and* the many other sources that

provide information about his date of birth and age. Each source is cited in a footnote or endnote. You would also discuss any conflicting evidence to demonstrate why you reject it. For simplicity's sake in our example, the one contradictory birth date statement came from the family Bible. The parish register information holds more evidentiary weight for you than the Bible entry after your due examination of the two sources, the information, and *all* the evidence together. You can say the evidence points to a confusion between baptismal date and birth date by the person who wrote the Bible entry. You will show that the sum of the evidence substantially and credibly supports the May date of birth rather than June.

Too often, conclusions are drawn before sufficient sources have been sought for relevant information and evidence. If we fail to research as many sources as possible, someone else will come across a source or sources with evidence that could overturn a premature conclusion. As Mills states: "Any relevant record that goes unexamined is a land mine waiting to explode our premature theories. If we know that potentially relevant records exist, we should use them."[5]

In our case example, thorough research would not ignore the availability of more sources. Some twentieth-century censuses have a column for precise date of birth. Robert's cemetery stone or potential newspaper obituary might offer somewhat new or variant information. His marriage record could give his age. He could have been in the right time and place for military service. Sources that refer to his parents or siblings or spouse may reveal unsuspected clues about Robert's birth. The list would go on extensively to all sources, original or derivative, that might yield relevant information and evidence.

Examples of proof summaries and proof arguments can be found in *The BCG Genealogical Standards Manual* and on the Board for Certification of Genealogists' website at *www.bcgcertification.org* and in scholarly journals. You can benefit from studying how others work from sources to information to evidence and conclusion.

The sources that provide information relevant to answering one question or addressing one hypothesis usually contain information relevant to accompanying research questions. While concentrating on Robert Kent's date of birth, we may have parallel questions or hypotheses about identifying his *place* of birth, the names of his parents, and so the process moves on.

Genealogical Proof Standard

Our small case followed a fairly simple research problem. Now we look at the Genealogical Proof Standard that sets out the measures we strive for. First, a wee bit of history: In those frequent situations where direct evidence was lacking or the evidence conflicted, the phrase **preponderance of evidence** (POE) was used by genealogists in the latter part of the twentieth century. The phrase applied to weighing the assembled evidence. POE was advocated by Stevenson (see Reading and Reference), borrowing from rules of evidence in civil and common law courts, where heirship cases are heard, as well as numerous other civil actions. However, a preponderance requires merely a *slight* balance one way or the other and is not strong enough to reflect credible, satisfactory genealogical conclusions. This is not just a semantic viewpoint. You should feel confident that you have made the maximum effort to support any assertion or argument you make. Research does not stop when only one piece of evidence tips the balance in favour of a conclusion.

Another degree of proof in civil cases, called "clear and convincing evidence," seemed more applicable to genealogy. Nevertheless, this legal term does not have a universal standard in all jurisdictions, so how could genealogists agree on a required amount or level of evidence? In contrast, the rules of evidence in criminal cases require a judge or jury to be convinced beyond a reasonable doubt. This much stronger phrase is rarely seen in genealogical arguments simply because it implies absolute certainty. Conclusions drawn from our evidence are always open to future re-interpretation in the light of new sources and information.

In the 1990s, dedicated genealogists began to question the borrowing of courtroom terminology, believing that self-demanding family researchers expect and deserve an exacting standard for proving identifications or relationships.

And thus the **Genealogical Proof Standard** (GPS) was developed as a stand-alone measurement for research excellence to meet the expectations of the genealogy community. The GPS posits five logical, progressive steps:[6]

1. We conduct a reasonably exhaustive search for all information that is or may be pertinent to the identity, relationship, event, or situation in question.
2. We collect a complete and accurate citation to the source or sources of each item of information we use.
3. We analyze and correlate the collected information to assess its quality as evidence.
4. We resolve any conflicts caused by items of evidence that contradict each other or are contrary to a proposed solution to the question.

5. We arrive at a soundly reasoned, coherently written, well-documented conclusion.

Additional Notes

- A *reasonably exhaustive search* applies to any project — simple or complex. The search for evidence extends beyond the immediate subject of our inquiry and the obvious sources. Information about the subject's parents, siblings, spouse(s), or associates may offer relevant evidence. Disregarding the potential contribution of additional relevant sources could result in missing a critical piece of evidence. A hasty conclusion based on limited sources could mean a weak assertion we can't adequately defend.

- A *written conclusion* is integral to the process. Many family historians find this step the most valuable and self-instructive.

- We use the word *proof* carefully and only when we have reached a convincing conclusion about the issue under discussion. Proof depends on *all* the assembled evidence with its attendant analysis, interpretation, and reasoning. Attorney Donn Devine, a leading genealogist points out:

  > As genealogists, we make a comprehensive search for all available evidence. We analyze its applicability to a particular person. If all factors align, we arrive at a conclusion of which we are convinced. If we've met the genealogical proof

standard, we can be reasonably sure that our conclusion will stand, even while we remain open to the possible discovery of new evidence. If our present evidence is convincing enough, we can state our finding without qualification. Otherwise, we are safer to qualify our conclusion as "probable," "possible," or "open to further study."[7]

In the Beginning

Most instructors in the field of genealogy will advise you, when you are starting a family project, to gather oral information from elderly relatives. Another early step is to check library catalogues and Internet material to see if one of the lines in your family history has already been "done." Both these steps are quite necessary at the beginning of your ancestral searches but, paradoxically, the steps involve mainly derivative sources. Often the information they produce is mixed or even faulty. Why, then, recommend these steps?

The answer should be clear by now. Both family and published sources can give essential starting points into your research path. Some family members are likely to have personal knowledge of events and relationships that may take you years to uncover through your own efforts. Published material, whether it has cited sources or not, can trigger a search for original documentation. Both steps are a beginning, not a conclusion, to research questions.

The advice comes with cautions. First, human memory can forget or confuse names, dates, and places of the past. Also, families may recall only the "good" things about the deceased and choose to remain silent about scandal and social stigma.

Censored or exaggerated, the stories could be coloured by any motive — personal, social, religious, or legal — for obscuring or changing the facts. You need to remind yourself not to perpetuate incomplete recollections or imperfectly remembered events by accepting them as unchallenged facts.

Second, published family histories are the work of someone else. They come in many shapes and forms — privately or commercially printed books, ornate family charts, compiled genealogies. It is possible that you can find material written about one of your own families. Published references are definitely exciting and useful discoveries, but are not to be accepted at face value. By hunting down the actual reference source you can make your own judgment about its value to your particular research project.

We don't want to repeat family hearsay or information from a publication without our own investigation. Even if an information item does have a source citation, we try to view that source ourselves whenever possible. Our examination of it might yield additional information, a different interpretation, and ultimately a different conclusion. Or possibly the cited source can be traced to secondary information being blindly repeated and copied until it was being accepted and cited as "fact."

For instance, a footnoted citation published in a widely praised local collection of historical essays looked like a promising lead to a source of family information. The footnote led to an older book that referred vaguely to an earlier, undated newspaper article. The hunt continued, with perseverance, to locate the article. The newspaper journalist wrote the article about his interview with the grandson of an immigrant pioneer, relating "facts" about the grandfather's life in Ireland. The information was two generations removed from the interviewee and heavily editorialized by the reporter. Each subsequent published version of the first article varied somewhat in the "facts."

In a search for the provenance of a derivative source, the current family historian must report all the inconsistencies. One of the dangers in relying on information from many derivative sources is that they could all lead back to a single, relatively unreliable source. The most impeccable procedure entails a hunt for the first or *original* source that started a chain of belief. If it leads to a now-inaccessible source (Irish grandfather has long since passed away), we report that. Then we must look to further sources for relevant evidence.

Citation of Sources

The final words in this section on standards of evidence deal briefly with the documentation of our sources of information. *Cite your sources* is a familiar phrase to family historians today. The emphasis here is on the importance and necessity of citations for serious research efforts. The sooner we acquire the habit of noting each source we consult, whether it contains information germane to the specific research task or not, the better off we are. (Be aware that *not* finding relevant information in a certain source, and noting that in writing, avoids needless guesswork and repetition of searches.)

Source citations are essential to our evaluation of evidence. Without them, we have no basis upon which to judge the reliability of any piece of information. They also show support for the statements we make. Moreover, interested readers should be able to judge for themselves the quality or value of that source. Lastly, the reader has the wherewithal to consult the same source or we ourselves can quickly return to it when need be.

A source citation needs enough detail to identify the source and where to locate it. The format of a citation is variable depending on the type of source involved and no one model "fits all." For instance, different *forms* of sources require slight differences in formatting a citation — the citation includes distinguishing among original documents, image copies, and derivative works. Consistency in citing each particular type of source is expected.

The basic elements of citations will include:

- the name of the creator, author, or compiler;
- the title of the overall source;
- further reference to a record series, chapter or article, item, or page number;
- publishing information, when applicable, to a printed work or website URL;
- the form in which the source was viewed, if applicable (microfilm, digital image, etc.); and
- reference to the subject or family, if applicable.

A superficial list of examples here would not do justice to the subject, especially when expert, specific guides are readily available for genealogical purposes. Explanatory information for examples requires much more space than possible here. The strongly recommended guides for details and a large variety of models are Elizabeth Shown Mills's *Evidence! Citation and Analysis for the Family Historian* and particularly *Evidence Explained: Citing History Sources from Artifacts and Cyberspace*. The first two chapters in the latter, "Fundamentals of Evidence Analysis" and "Fundamentals of Citation," are masterful descriptions for comprehension of the underlying foundations. For basic reference models to Internet sources, see the two handy laminated guides, *QuickSheet: Citing Online Historical Resources, Evidence! Style* and *QuickSheet: Citing Ancestry.com® Databases and Images, Evidence! Style.*

In 2007, Mills wrote:

> As researchers, we should continue to evaluate the credibility of every source against new evidence. To do that, our research notes must do more than merely name a source and cite its *location*. Our notes should also *describe* the source in sufficient detail that we, at any future point, can reconsider our evaluation. As writers, we owe our readers that same description, so that they can better assess the soundness of our judgment.[8]

Critical evaluation of sources and analysis of evidence continues each time we find new information. Those of us already deep into the accumulation of information may also benefit from revisiting our past research. Following the Genealogical Proof Standard, we may see where we can re-analyze evidence and revise conclusions we reached in previous years, made at a time when we had perhaps more enthusiasm than experience!

If and when sources do not produce satisfactory evidence to support a hypothesis, say so. And say why. Use proof arguments to explain conflicts or unresolved questions. By all means include family tales and memories in your history, as long as you indicate that they are apocryphal and as yet unverified. Future genealogists may be able to make advances, thanks to your clearly defined groundwork. Genealogy is a never-ending quest for truth, as close to the truth as we can reach. Today we have better access than ever to sources and finding aids. We owe it to ourselves, our families, and our fellow family historians to pass on the very best we can do.

Checklist of Genealogical Sources

Family Name _____ **Location** _____

1. Family Records
Personal/Family Records
__ Family Bibles
__ Oral traditions
__ Journals/diaries
__ Letters
__ Memorial cards
__ Scrapbooks
__ Photographs
__ Heirlooms
__ Farm records
__ Health/medical
__ Military files
__ Citizenship papers
__ S.I.N. cards
__ Account books
__ Employment records
__ Social Security cards
Certificates
__ Birth
__ Marriage
__ Death
__ Adoption
__ Baptism
__ Confirmation
__ Blessing
__ Graduation

__ Fraktur
__ Manumission
__ Divorce
School Records
__ Elementary
__ Secondary
__ Vocational
__ Trade
__ College
__ University
__ Private
__ Arts
__ Ladies Finishing
Insurance
__ Life
__ Automobile
__ Fire
__ Marine
__ Accident
__ Health
2. Vital Statistics
Vital Records
__ Births
__ Marriages
__ Deaths
__ Divorces
__ Adoptions

© RMB Genealogical Services 103–12140 Ninth Line, Stouffville, ON L4A 1L2 Canada tel. (905) 640-7391 fax (905) 640-9359 *ruth.burk@sympatico.ca*. The checklist may be photocopied for personal use by the purchaser of this book.

Checklist of Genealogical Sources

Family Name _____ **Location** _____

Marriage Records
__ Indexes
__ Banns
__ Bonds, Applications
__ Licences
__ Contracts
__ Minister's records
__ J.P.s' Returns

3. Compiled Sources
Genealogical Society of Utah Indexes
__ IGI
__ Ancestral File
__ Family Register
__ FGRA – Family Group Records Archives
__ Temple Index Bureau
Genealogical Periodicals
__ Indexes
__ Queries
__ Genealogies
__ Source extracts
__ Historical articles
__ Society newsletters
Genealogical Directories
__ GRD (Worldwide)
__ Big "R" (British)

Printed Sources
__ Family histories
__ Genealogies
__ Biographies
__ Pedigrees
__ Ahnentafel charts
__ County/local histories
__ City directories
__ Telephone directories
__ County atlas
__ County maps
__ Voters' lists
__ Cemetery transcriptions
__ School yearbooks

4. Public Sources
Canadian Census
__ Indexes
__ 1828
__ 1842
__ 1848
__ 1851/2
__ 1861
__ 1871
__ Agricultural schedules
__ Mortality schedules
__ 1881
__ 1891

Checklist of Genealogical Sources

Family Name _____ **Location** _____

__ 1901

__ 1911

__ Address schedules

__ 1916

U.S. Federal Census

__ Indexes

__ 1790

__ 1800

__ 1810

__ 1820

__ 1830

__ 1840

__ 1850

__ 1860

__ 1870

__ 1880

__ 1900

__ 1910

__ 1920

__ 1930

__ Agricultural schedules

__ Mortality schedules

__ Revolutionary War
   Survivors

__ Union Army Survivors

State/Local Census

__

__

Land Records

__ Grantee index

__ Grantor index

__ Abstract index

__ Deeds

__ Mortgages

__ Surveys

__ Land petitions

__ Patents, grants

__ Heir & devisee

__ Leases

__ Wills

__ Homestead records

__ Bounty lands

Probate Records

__ Indexes

__ Wills

__ Administrations

__ Inventories

__ Bonds

__ Settlements

__ Packets

__ Estate files

__ Copy books

Court Records

__ Dockets

Checklist of Genealogical Sources

Family Name _____ **Location** _____

__ Minutes
__ Orders, decrees
__ Judges' bench books
__ Quarter Session Courts
__ Judgments
__ Case files
__ Indexes
__ Registers
__ Chancery proceedings

Court Related Records
__ Sheriff
__ Police
__ Jail
__ Jury
__ Lawyers' Briefs
__ Justice of Peace

Tax Records
__ Poll tax
__ Personal property
__ Assessment/Collectors' rolls
__ Real estate
__ School
__ Poor rate
__ Tax exemptions

Military Sources
__ Service files
__ Pensions

__ Bounty awards
__ Discharges
__ Muster rolls
__ Regimental diaries
__ Awards/honours

Immigrant Records
__ Passenger lists
__ Passports
__ Vaccination certificates
__ Alien registration cards
__ Change of name
__ Oaths of allegiance
__ Register of voters
__ Logbooks
__ Naturalization
__ Citizenship papers
__ Customs records
__ Immigrant aid societies
__ Consular records
__ Border crossings

Cemetery Records
__ Burial registers from the
   cemetery office
__ Sextons
__ Monuments
__ Tombstones
__ Plats

Checklist of Genealogical Sources

Family Name _____ **Location** _____

__ Deeds

__ Perpetual care

__ Funds

__ Memorials

__ Gifts

5. Private Sources

Religious Records

__ Birth

__ Christening/Naming

__ Bar/Bat mitzvah

__ Confirmation

__ Ordination

__ Marriage

__ Banns

__ Divorce

__ Annulment

__ Death

__ Burial

__ Circumcision

__ Admissions

__ Removals

__ Disciplinary proceedings

__ Subscription lists

__ Membership lists

__ Minister's records

__ Religious school

__ Mission reports

Newspapers

__ Indexes

__ Births

__ Marriages

__ Deaths

__ Anniversaries

__ Obituaries

__ Advertisements

__ Unclaimed mail

__ Local news

Legal Notices

__ Probates

__ Auctions

__ Divorces

__ Bankruptcies

__ Forced sales

__ Court claims

__ Convictions

Employment

__ Indentures

__ Apprenticeships

__ Licences

__ Pensions

__ Service awards

__ Personnel files

__ Account books

__ Company histories

Checklist of Genealogical Sources

Family Name _____ **Location** _____

Mortuary Records
__ Burial Registers
__ Funeral cards
__ Funeral books

Institutional Records
__ Charities
__ Hospitals
__ Convents
__ Seminaries
__ Libraries
__ Schools
__ Historical societies
__ Genealogical societies
__ Mission societies
__ Orphan societies
__ Reunion societies
__ Children's Aid societies
__ Lunatic asylums

Collections
__ Indexes
__ Personal papers
__ Correspondence
__ Surname files
__ Biographies
__ Inscriptions
__ DAR
__ UEL

__ Business records
__ Oral histories
__ WPA projects
__ Photographs

Genealogical Websites
__ Ancestry.com
__ ScotlandsPeople.com
__ Findmypast.com
__ Worldvitalrecords.com
__ OCFA
__ GenWeb (locality of interest)
__ JewishGen.org

CHAPTER 3

Learning and Practice

Q: How can I stay in touch with new techniques and resources as I work on my own particular families? How can I feel assured that I am applying sound genealogical principles?

A: This chapter has suggestions for continuing your learning and developing good practices. Formal and informal venues offer expert speakers on skillbuilding and many educational topics. We learn by reading exemplary genealogical journals. Peer-testing systems exist for measuring your competence. Learning to write your proof arguments and conclusions can be expanded to family biographies and research experiences to practise your own skills. Publishing in society periodicals is always a rewarding exercise.

Self-improvement and Education

Most of us may be content to expand our knowledge by attending local meetings, workshops, or seminars. This is where membership in a genealogical society is so valuable: it tells you when and where nearby educational events are being held and how the overall themes or specific talks can interest you. Fellowship in a society can result in numerous new contacts and ideas. While some of us are prepared to plan a vacation to visit ancestral sites, why not plan similar time to register for a major genealogy conference farther afield or take one of the guided tours to a resource centre like the Family History Library? A side benefit derived from such a conference or guided tour, besides the research value, is the social interaction with fellow genealogists.

However, not everyone has the opportunity of attending genealogy courses or conferences. Perhaps there is no active society in your town or no courses offered locally. Distance education has grown by leaps and bounds, especially through the Internet. New media and forms of communication are being used with great imagination and technical support. Keeping in touch with genealogical developments is much easier now with online communications and prevents working in a vacuum.

Online and Home Study Courses

Finding a website and registration information can be done by simply making selective online searches, but is best when you have a recommendation from someone who took a course. By discussing the experience, you are better able to choose the institution or courses you want. Some of the more well-known institutions, with international instructors, are listed here. Inevitably, some of the information changes as time goes by, so the comments are general.

National Institute of Genealogical Studies
Continuing Education
University of St. Michael's College at University of Toronto
81 St. Mary Street
Toronto, ON M5S 1J4
(416) 861-0165 or 1-800-580-0165
www.genealogicalstudies.com

The National Institute operates in conjunction with the Continuing Education Division of St. Michael's and is a fully online program with a multitude of courses. Most courses are also available by correspondence. Certificate programs are offered on three levels — Basic, Intermediate, and Advanced — with a Professional Learning Certificate in Genealogical Studies for graduates completing the full requirements. Methodology is one required series. Departments include Canadian, English, American, Irish, Scottish, and German genealogy.

NGS American Genealogy: A Home Study Course
3108 Columbia Pike, Suite 300
Arlington, VA 22204-4304
(703) 525-0050 or 1-800-473-0060
www.ngsgenealogy.org

The National Genealogical Society has always been a leader in education, now offering several multiple-lesson online courses. *American Genealogy: A Home Study Course* is their excellent 16-lesson certificate course, available in a series of three CDs. You can choose to be graded or not, working at your own pace within a specified period. Details of the courses should be consulted at their website. The course is most recommended for U.S. residents with its emphasis on American sources.

Akamai University

193 Kino'ole Street
Hilo, HI 96720
(877) 934-8793
www.akamaiuniversity.us

Akamai has an ambitious online program for undergraduate and master's degrees in genealogical studies. This is another important step for recognition of genealogy and family history as legitimate post-secondary degree programs. At the website, see "Education and Literacy" under "Degree Programs" for entry and degree requirements, and the transfer of credits. The courses are set at an academic level, appealing to practising and would-be professional genealogists.

Pharos Teaching & Tutoring Ltd.

3 Beaford Grove
London SW20 9LB
United Kingdom
+44 (208) 542-6552
www.pharostutors.com

Mainly designed for those with British family interests, the online courses are "self-assisted study" with instructor interaction. Offerings include English, Welsh, Scottish, and Irish topics, plus research strategies and writing skills. An American course is also available, with Caribbean Family History an unusual and, perhaps, unique offering.

Brigham Young University

Family History Certificate Program Administrator
Independent Study

206 HCEB
P.O. Box 21514
Provo, UT 84602-1514
ce.byu.edu

BYU has a Certificate Program in Family History (Genealogy) at a post-secondary level with American or British options. Non-credit "Free Web Courses" are also available, found at the BYU website in the Independent Study section. Each of the free family history courses consists of several self-monitored lessons at an introductory level. They work with PDF (Adobe Acrobat) files and updated browsers.

Boston University
One Silber Way
Boston, MA 02215
(617) 353-4636
professional.bu.edu/cpe/Genealogy.asp

Boston is the latest university to offer a quality course for a Certificate in Genealogical Research. In five modules, expert instructors impart essential skills training, covering "genealogical principles, techniques, and core competencies." Started as a classroom-only program, it is intended to go online in the fall of 2009.

The Institute of Heraldic and Genealogical Studies
79-82 Northgate
Canterbury, Kent CT1 1BA
U.K.
+44 (122) 776-5617
www.ihgs.ac.uk

Founded in 1961, the institute is an independent charitable trust offering a variety of studies in family history and heraldic research. The popular and comprehensive home studies program is accredited by the U.K. Open and Distance Learning Quality Council. Students have the option of examination at different levels for a certificate, diploma, or licentiateship. On-site courses are also available all year long as well as residential weekends or week-long programs.

Virtual Study Groups

Online study groups are a welcome twenty-first-century addition to learning. Those who join are asked to commit themselves over a certain period of time. The no-fee programs usually involve concentration on a particular resource with regular online discussions appropriate to each topic. The great advantage, of course, is that virtually anyone in the world with an Internet connection, no matter how isolated geographically, can take part in the interaction. Study groups for serious continuing education and skillbuilding have prompted enthusiastic feedback and will no doubt greatly increase. Members may take turns moderating the chat and preparing questions or assignments. Some groups also include peer review of the assignments, and some may have a credentialed mentor to monitor discussions. The most recommended virtual study groups at this time follow models set up by qualified professionals. For more information, subscribe to (and inquire at) *TRANSITIONAL-GENEALOGISTS-FORUM-request@rootsweb.com*. Intermediate or advanced readers may want to visit *progenstudy.org*, geared more to those developing a professional business.

Institutes (Personal Attendance)

The opportunity for intensive week-long institutes away from home has also expanded. Some institutes are planned for summer months when many people can take vacation time. Courses by well-known instructors are geared to different levels of research experience, and are usually limited in the number of participants for maximum attention. Online registration is usually available.

National Institute on Genealogical Research
P.O. Box 118
Greenbelt, MD 20768-0118
www.rootsweb.com/~natgenin

The NIGR is over fifty years old now, its roots firmly embedded with the U.S. National Archives and Records Administration in Washington, D.C., where courses take place. As can be expected, this week-long institute concentrates on the archives' resources and is intended for experienced, not beginning, researchers. Two scholarships are available for NIGR.

Institute of Genealogy and Historical Research
Samford University Library
800 Lakeshore Drive
Birmingham, AL 35229-7008
(205) 726-4447
www.samford.edu/schools/ighr

Samford is another treasured summer learning centre, with "academically and professionally oriented courses," recommended by the Board for Certification of Genealogists. On-campus housing is provided. The topnotch instructors give training not only in sources, but also advanced classes in strategies, techniques, and critical analysis. Each year they offer almost a dozen streams to choose from, but enrollment fills up fast after the January program announcement.

Salt Lake Institute of Genealogy

P.O. Box 1144
Salt Lake City, UT 84110
1-888-463-6842
www.infouga.org

The Utah Genealogical Association sponsors a week in January with reasonable hotel accommodation in Salt Lake City. Here you have hands-on access to the Family History Library with experienced instructors for American sources and problem-solving. Courses and sessions for other countries may be available from year to year. The association also sponsors an annual conference.

The British Institute

International Society for British Genealogy and Family History
P.O. Box 350459
Westminster, CO 80035-0459
isbgfh.org

Held annually in Salt Lake City, The British Institute is a week-long series of sessions on various geographic and topic source material for England, Ireland, Wales, and Scotland with international instructors. The sponsoring society, ISBGFH, also offers membership and newsletters to keep current with British Isles news. Check their website for Institute announcements.

Certification and Accreditation

Certification by an independent, peer-testing organization is not to be confused with a *certificate,* which is a formal acknowledgement that a certain educational program of courses has been completed. Certifying bodies are traditionally independent from any societies and do not offer educational programs leading to their credentials. It is due largely to their efforts that research standards have been developed and promulgated. They are not "membership" societies. One earns the credential through individual demonstration of abilities. Certifying organizations have newsletters or, sometimes, email lists or forums for their associates. A list of qualified associates will be available on their websites or in print form.

Accreditation or certification in the field of genealogy has been solidly in place for well over forty years. Genealogists and family historians who wish to develop an income-earning career are the obvious candidates. However, don't be misled that "going into business" is a requirement for the process. Some find certification a complement to a related type of job, for example, librarians and archivists who serve the public in a records centre. Volunteers who answer inquiries for a local society or historical centre, society officers, those who publish newsletters, or act as a family association genealogist are examples of those who want professional recognition. Many people apply to undergo the testing with no intention of seeking clients or becoming hired researchers. Why would you consider this? Here are some of the reasons given by family historians:

- To confirm my learning.
- To experience personal challenge and satisfaction.
- To measure my skills.

- To learn to write clearly.
- To raise the personal bar, push beyond my usual scope.
- To clarify my research strengths and weaknesses.
- To know I give the best to my family history.
- To be among the achievers.

Earned genealogical credentials (e.g. CG, CGL, or AG postnominals) after your name bespeak competence to the general public and achievement among the genealogy community. Successful applicants are asked to sign and adhere to a code of ethics. Here are the main agencies:

Board for Certification of Genealogists
P.O. Box 14291
Washington, DC 20044
www.bcgcertification.org

The Board, established in 1964, certifies successful applicants in the research category (Certified Genealogist or CG) and the teaching category (Certified Genealogical Lecturer or CGL). After submitting a preliminary application, applicants will receive the *Application Guide* and *The BCG Genealogical Standards Manual*. Completing the requirements from home can take up to one year, with some allowance for extensions. The Board's goal is to determine that you meet the essential standards of research methodology, evidence analysis, kinship determination, and reporting, as well as know the sources of your area. The judges' remarks and recommendations assist you in improving your skills. To retain certification, you are required to make five-year renewals by submitting work samples of continued excellence and professional growth. The BCG website has expanded to become as helpful as possible to potential applicants. There you will find FAQs, a host of skillbuilding articles, and a "Test Your Skills" page.

International Commission for the Accreditation of Professional Genealogists

P.O. Box 970204
Orem, UT 84097-0204
1-866-813-6729
www.icapgen.org

In 1964 the Family History Department of the Church of Jesus Christ of Latter-day Saints (LDS) set up a program for professional accreditation, when it could no longer accommodate heavy demands for research requests in its Family History Library (FHL) collections in Salt Lake City. In 2000, the accreditation program was transferred to "ICAPGen," which continues the same basic examination formats. The sole category is Accredited Genealogist or AG. The program tests applicants for many world geographic localities and some specialty topic areas. It is possible to become accredited in more than one specialty. Major requirements on the application are evidence of no less than one thousand hours of research work and a four-generation lineage involving pre-1900 records in the chosen specialty area. A written examination and an extensive oral examination will follow. Thorough knowledge of FHL holdings is expected, as well as relevant local material not available in the FHL resources. Formerly conducted only in Salt Lake City, examination sites have been extended to additional cities.

Genealogical Institute of the Maritimes

P.O. Box 36022
Canada Post Postal Office

5675 Spring Garden Road
Halifax, NS B3J 1G0
nsgna.ednet.ns.ca/gim/index.html

The Institute, established in 1983, has two types of certification for research in Atlantic Canada: Certified Genealogist (Canada) and Genealogical Record Searcher (Canada). The postnominals are CG(C) and GRS(C). Applicants are initially rated on a point system and work samples. Upon favourable recommendations by three evaluators, candidates are then expected to attend an examination and an oral interview at a site in the Maritimes. Procedures can be conducted in either French or English and research pertains to the four Atlantic provinces of Canada.

Bureau québécois d'attestation de compétence en généalogie
c/o Fédération québécoise des sociétés de généalogie
Case postale 9454
Sainte-Foy, QC G1V 4B8
www.federationgenealogie.qc.ca (see "BQACG")

The Bureau was created in 1990 by the fédération québécoise, an alliance of francophone genealogical societies, with representation from the Archives nationales du Québec. The testing is entirely *en français* with requirements focusing on research in the province of Quebec and possibly leading back to France. Three categories are described:

maître généalogiste agréé (MGA)
généalogiste recherchiste agréé (GRA)
généalogiste de filiation agréé (GFA)

Three judges will evaluate an applicant on both written and oral examinations. The participation of the Archives nationales du Québec in this program is notable in that successful candidates are recognized and approved as leaders in their field by official keepers of records.

Lineage Societies

Lineage societies have a special place in the genealogical field. The criterion for membership is to document *direct-line* ascent to an ancestor who fulfills an "exclusive" type of requirement. The submitted application must demonstrate the applicant's careful linkage of each generation, and usually must also prove that the targeted ancestor fits the expected requirement. The well-known societies briefly outlined here, and various other such groups, support serious research for their objectives. Lineage groups have been created for descent from pioneers in some specific regions, from royalty, or even for perhaps more frivolous goals. Websites and information can be found by Internet searching. The Canadian Heraldic Authority is mentioned as a resource strongly related to lineage and genealogy.

United Empire Loyalists' Association of Canada
Dominion Headquarters
50 Baldwin Street, Suite 202
Toronto, ON M5T 1L4
(416) 591-1783
www.uelac.org

The only hereditary society in Canada is the United Empire Loyalists' Association of Canada. The association was formed in

1914 from smaller existing groups, to honour ancestors loyal to the British cause during the American Revolutionary War. The governor of British North America in 1789, Lord Dorchester, declared a Resolution with an accompanying Form of Militia Roll as recognition of those who "adhered to the Unity of Empire" by creating the initials UE to follow their names. Dorchester deliberately extended this privilege to "... all their Children and their Descendants by either sex." Upon approval of a well-researched application, a certificate and regular membership are given to someone who "bears allegiance to the Crown," meaning to the British monarch as head of state. Associate and affiliate memberships are also offered.

The UELAC has clear historical criteria to describe Loyalist ancestors, and that includes original members of the Six Nations who left the American colonies at the same time. The association provides guidelines for acceptable sources and proof, supplemented by branch genealogists and libraries, and its main website. Members receive the semi-annual journal *Loyalist Gazette*. Any interested party can freely subscribe to the weekly electronic newsletter *Loyalist Trails*.

General Society of Mayflower Descendants
P.O. Box 3297
Plymouth, MA 02361-3297
(508) 746-3188
www.themayflowersociety.com
www.rootsweb.com/~canms/canada.html (Canadian site)

Members of the General Society of Mayflower Descendants, established in 1897 in the United States, must provide evidence of their lineage in each generation from one of the known Pilgrim passengers on the vessel *Mayflower* that landed at Plymouth,

Massachusetts, in December 1620. *Mayflower* descendants to the fourth or fifth generation have been well-documented in the Society's *Five Generation Project*, so potential members often need only pursue their own research to one of those descendants. The Society historian will advise and assist each applicant while the website provides valuable tips on research and documentation.

Numerous *Mayflower* family societies exist throughout the United States, and the Canadian Society of Mayflower Descendants was formed in 1980. The General Society supports a historical museum and library in connection with their headquarter offices. *The Mayflower Quarterly* goes to all members with news and featured articles, also available by subscription to non-members.

Daughters of the American Revolution
1776 D Street NW
Washington, DC 20006
(202) 628-1776
www.dar.org

Sons of the American Revolution
1000 South Fourth Street
Louisville, KY 40203
(502) 589-1776
www.sar.org

A woman's lineal descent from a Patriot of the Revolutionary War period is the requirement for DAR membership. The DAR library in Washington is renowned for its vast collection of historical and genealogical resources, with an online catalogue and in-house databases. The large, active organization also supports a museum and many chapters. The Sons of the American Revolution is a similar lineage society for men with equal emphasis on patriotism.

Both provide worksheets for the preliminary application to assist with lineage tracing and identifying the appropriate ancestor.

Chief Herald of Canada
Canadian Heraldic Authority
Rideau Hall
Ottawa, ON K1A 0A1
(613) 993-8200 or 1-800-465-6890
www.gg.ca/heraldry/index_e.asp

The Canadian Heraldic Authority is not precisely a lineage society, but is of interest to anyone with connections to an armigerous line. The Authority was established in 1988, with the same royal prerogative as Her Majesty's two ancient heraldic offices in the United Kingdom: the College of Arms in London and the Court of the Lord Lyon in Edinburgh. While a large part of Canadian heraldry is occupied with institutional and corporate arms, many individuals have also had personal arms designed and granted — any Canadian citizen is eligible to make the request. A procedure guide and more information are available on the website, or alternatively, contact the Authority or the Royal Heraldry Society of Canada (*www.hsc.ca*).

The Authority maintains the "Public Register of Arms, Flags and Badges of Canada" as a record of the registrations and grants they have sanctioned, available on its website. A personal grant of arms is unique to one recipient, and cannot lawfully be assumed by anyone else. In addition, the CHA keeps separate genealogical files for claims "to bear arms by lawful descent from an original recipient."[9] This means that their files may contain information on the receipt of arms from another recognized Authority. For example, a grant or inheritance from Britain or Europe may be registered with the CHA.

Writing and Publishing

Writing family history is the ultimate step for communicating your work in a permanent form and expressing the results of your research, including the resolution of sometimes conflicting evidence. Let's emphasize again: reading case studies in journals and magazines and well-written family histories will familiarize you with how others do it.

Some family historians will say they can't write. Are you one of them? The objective of this section is to encourage the timid to practise writing incrementally. Writing may not come easily to everyone, but solving a problem is what most of us thrive on. Continual investigation and challenges are integral to the very nature of genealogy and why it keeps a hold on us.

In the chapter about the Genealogical Proof Standard, writing was discussed as the means of expressing a genealogical conclusion that you drew from the analysis of collected evidence. Your creation of this proof summary, or a proof argument, demonstrates support of your original hypothesis or the solution to your question. Considering the mental process you went through to reach a conclusion, you have the wherewithal to convey it in writing. You can also consider that connecting your thought process to an orderly written approach is merely the next step in a natural progression. Many family historians find this ultimate step in the GPS process the most valuable and instructive learning experience.

Outlining the pieces of evidence for your conclusion in point form could be a way to begin. Maybe you have twelve points that all agree, so your summary is straightforward. Or, more likely, some evidence contradicts the majority, so you describe your reasons for not accepting it. Proof summaries from brief to complex are of interest to other family historians. The sources you used, the information they contained, and how you analyzed the evidence can be interesting and instructional for others. Before you know it, you have a paragraph or a page to be proud of. We cheer you on. This can be the beginning of *writing* the family history.

Creating a biography about one ancestor is another good way to practise writing. It can be as small as a paragraph or grow to impressive proportions. Sharing your experience and seeing your efforts in print will boost your self-assurance. Society newsletters and journals nearly always welcome new material. Societies with large memberships often have two levels of publication — a newsletter with short articles, and a more formal periodical with lengthier articles. The commercial magazines that circulate in North America are another publishing avenue. Familiarize yourself with the publications for their variations in style and content. It is always wise to inquire first, with a note about your intended topic.

Blogging has become a favoured medium for some family historians. Various providers offer free space and the setup is not difficult, even for those with low-tech competence. Feedback on the site is not necessarily comprehensive or constructive with regard to style, but blog posts can lead to contact with new and knowledgeable correspondents about your subject matter.

The end goal for most genealogists is to produce a family history. Publishing is an adventure in itself, with several options. Doing it yourself on a website is almost as popular as producing a paper-based result. The capability of including maps, charts, photographs, and other illustrations is always a consideration. You may choose to work with a knowledgeable printer or publisher, possibly even with a designer who can create a professional appearance. Or you may be working with a computer program from which you can print out copies on demand. Genealogical software is a good companion as a database for storing your accumulating information. A collection of family charts and related documents may be all you want to preserve, although the cookie-cutter format of many software "reports" is not as compelling or attractive as a family history written with the flexibility of a word-processing program. Now it is possible to combine the two to best effect. Please see the recommended publications in Reading and Reference for further guidance. A completed family history or any other kind of written family project deserves a place in an appropriate society library or public library.

As you gain writing experience, you may want to branch out to more demanding venues with a case study in problem-solving. Asking a colleague or friend to review and proofread your final draft before sending it off is also good practice. Thoughtful editors with enough time will offer constructive advice on submissions from new authors. If your proposed article includes two or more generations of a family, you should definitely accompany it with a recognized or standard genealogical format to display and summarize the individuals involved. Some periodicals have their own authors' style sheet. Editors of major periodicals send new submissions to peer reviewers for comments that get passed back to you.

Experienced authors frequently aspire to publication in scholarly journals. The few periodicals below are mentioned because they regularly contain articles on identification issues and analysis of evidence or several generations of a compiled genealogy. Numerous other journals are equally prestigious, with perhaps a narrower geographic focus. Learning form and style is reinforced by familiarity. For genealogical writing at its best, you can do no better than to subscribe to and emulate the following:

NGS Quarterly (National Genealogical Society)[10]
NGSQ Editorial Office
Gallaudet Research Center, HMB S-439

Gallaudet University
800 Florida Avenue NE
Washington, DC 22202-3695
www.ngsgenealogy.org

The American Genealogist
P.O. Box 398
Demorest, GA 30535-0398
www.americangenealogist.com

Crossroads (Utah Genealogical Association)
P.O. Box 1144
Salt Lake City, UT 84110
infouga.org

The New England Historical Genealogical Register
101 Newbury Street
Boston, MA 02116-3087
www.nehgs.org

The Genealogist
Picton Press
P.O. Box 1347
Rockland, ME 04841
www.fasg.org/TheGenealogist.html

In striving to meet research standards of excellence, we can produce works of value for family, friends, and colleagues. Moreover, we help to increase general public awareness of this fascinating field. Writing and publishing the results of a carefully analyzed project adds to a serious body of literature that academic scholars could envy.

Namen	Aeltern	Tauffzeugen Pathen
Hans geb. 3 Jan. 1798. getauft 16. Febr. ej. a.	James Hennessy et Christina.	Parentes
Stephan 21 May. 1797.	Abel Gilbert et un. j. Blandine	Caleb Gilbert und Nancy Gilbert
Margaretha 8 Dec. 1797.	James Falkner et un. j. Catarina	Christoph Hagermann et un. j. Höhe
Luisa und Rebeka 28 Aug. 1797.	John Wiest et un. j. Margret	Luisi Roseleth und Margret Lot
	William Smith et un. j. Mariane	John Lot und George Ariens

CHAPTER 4

Some Illustrated Examples

Lutheran Church Register

Not all early church records were in English, as shown on this page of a register kept by a German-speaking clergyman in the Midland District of Upper Canada. A religious register is usually an original source that we expect to provide primary information and direct evidence of baptismal (in this example) dates with children's and parents' names. The first entry postdates the others, but is still direct evidence of that event. The minister sometimes recorded a date of birth as well as baptism. The parents and godparents are named, but not their places of residence. Notice that not all the names are Germanic, perhaps indicating a lack of English-speaking clergy in the area.

Evangelical Lutheran Congregation of the Townships of Camden East, Ernestown, Fredericksburg, and Richmond, "Baptisms, Marriages and Communions, 1791–1850," unpaginated (1798); Archives of Ontario microfilm MS 138.

SCHEDULE A.—BIRTHS.

County of *Huron*   Division of *Seaforth*

No.		**015206** No. 1	**015207** No. 2
When Born.		December 16th 1887	September 29th 1887
Name.		Charlie Reginald Andrews	(still born)
Sex—Male or Female.		M.	Female
Name and Surname of Father.		Walter Andrews	Joseph Brownell
Name and Maiden Surname of Mother.		Catharine Mullins	Harriet Charlesworth
Rank or Profession of Father.		Butcher	Merchant
Signature, Description and Residence of Informant.		Catharine M. Andrews, Seaford	J. Brownell Seaforth
When Registered.		January 31st 1888	January 5th 1888
of Acheur.		Wm Hanover M.D.	J. Campbell M.D.
Signature of Registrar.		Wm Elliott	Wm Elliott
REMARKS.			

Ontario Birth

The provincial registrations of vital events are official government records. Although they are clerk's copies, not original sources, they carry legal authority. A person with firsthand knowledge would have to report the event within a specified time period. Most often in the nineteenth century, the father was charged with registering a birth. Stillborn children were also registered. In this case, the mother appears to be the informant about six weeks after the event. The mother's birth surname was recorded on a child's birth registration as a fairly regular practice in Ontario and is usually considered primary information and direct evidence of her identity.

Charlie Reginald Andrews, Ontario birth registration 015206 (1888); Archives of Ontario microfilm MS 929 reel 88.

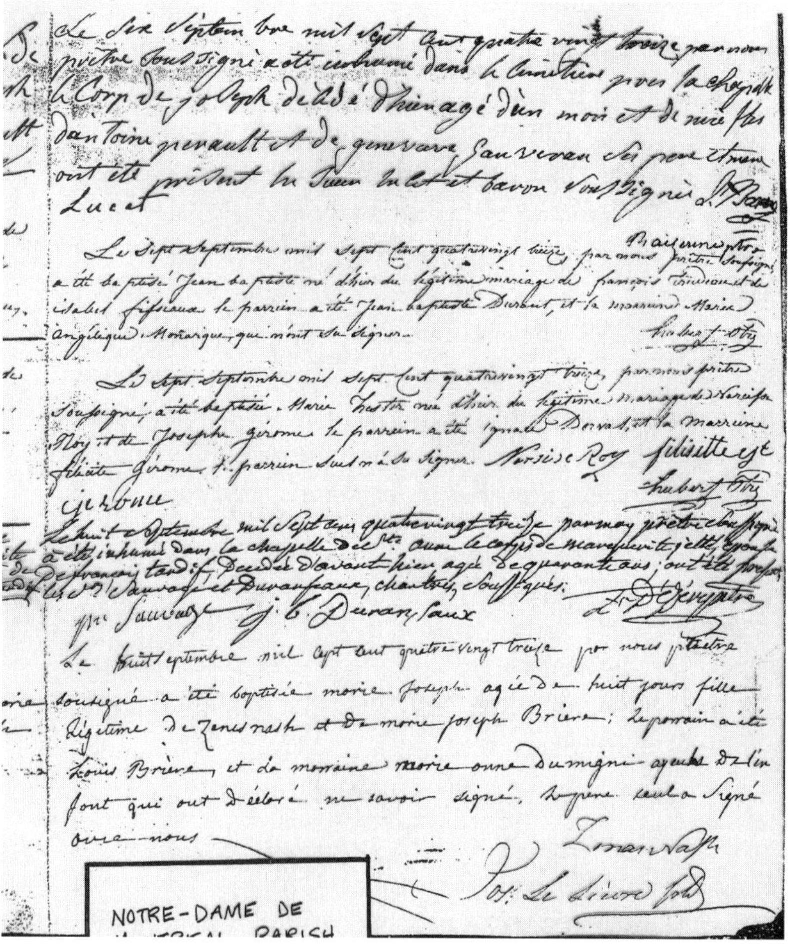
NOTRE-DAME DE

Montreal Church Register

The events are chronological and appear to be entered in a timely way by the various priests. Many churches first began recording baptisms, marriages, and burials all in one register. Later, separate registers would be maintained for different sacraments. The third entry here was for a burial of a one-month-old child whose parents were present and named. In the baptismal entries, the full name of each parent is given and the godparents. The parents' names are primary information and direct evidence of the child's relationship to them.

"Quebec Vital and Church Records (Drouin Collection), 1621–1967," digital image, Ancestry.ca (*www.ancestry.ca*: accessed 22 September 2009), entry for Joseph Perault, 6 September 1793; citing Basilique Notre-Dame de Montréal, Baptêmes, Mariages et Sépultures, Montréal, Québec.

St. Clements Church
ST. CLEMENTS - ONTARIO

✝

Certificate of Baptism

I certify that

according to the Register of Baptisms at St. Clements Church, St. Clements, Ontario

John Henry Kurz
(NAME)

born *Oct 26,* 19 *1847*

the child of *John Kurz (a blacksmith in Bridgeport*

and *Mary Fink*

was baptised on *Nov. 21,* 19 *1847*

W. L. Ryan
(Signature of Priest)

(SEAL)

August 26, 19 *86*
(Date Issued)

"Unless a man be born again of water and the Holy Spirit, he cannot enter into the kingdom of God." —(John III : 5)

N.B.—This certificate not valid in matters de quibus in CC. 1021, ¶1; 1363, ¶1, ¶2; 544, ¶1, Codicis Iuris Canonici.

Godparents were Henry Summer and his wife Christine, née Shratz

Baptismal Certificate

Information on this certificate was extracted from the original register more than one hundred years after the event occurred. The certificate is a derivative source by genealogical standards, although the evidence directly answers when the subject was born. Since the birth and baptism occurred well before civil registration was established, the certificate would be acceptable as sufficient proof of identity for government or legal purposes. It may not be possible ever to see the original register from which this came — many churches wish to protect the privacy of other entries on the same page as your ancestor. This document provides both birth and baptismal dates, and the birth names of the parents with the father's occupation and residence. The names of the godparents may be clues to family relationships. John Kurz's status as a village blacksmith may open new research avenues for the descendant.

St. Clements Catholic Church (St. Clements, Ontario), "Certificate of Baptism," John Henry Kurz (1847), issued 1986.

MARRIAGES

County of _Perth_   Division of _Township of Downie_

		No. 1	No. 2	No. 3
		Surname first	Surname first	Surname first
Name of Groom	1	Thompson J. C.	Wilson John Albert	
Age	2	38	26	
Date of Marriage	3	Sep. 19, 1906. Tp. Downie	Sep. 11, 1906	
Place of Marriage	4	Township of Downie	Township of Downie	
Residence when Married	5	Virden Manitoba	Vondon? Ont	
Place of Birth	6	County of Simcoe	London	
Bachelor or Widower	7	W	B.	
Occupation	8	Farmer	Cooper	
Name of Father	9	Thompson John	Wilson Francis	
Maiden Name of Mother	10	Stevenson Anna	McNeill Catherine	
Religious Denomination	11	P.		
Name of Bride	12	Fichling Eliza	Durward Minnie Ann	
Age	13	25	24	
Residence when Married	14	Tp. Downie	Tp. Downie	
Place of Birth	15	Tp. Downie	Tp. Downie	
Spinster or Widow	16	S	S	
Occupation	17	Farmer's daughter	Farmer's daughter	
Name of Father	18	Fichling Charles	Durward William	
Maiden Name of Mother	19	Willis Sarah Elinor	Thompson Elizabeth	
Religious Denomination	20	P.	P.	
Names and Residences of Witnesses	21	Anderson May Tonawanda Fichling Martha Downie	Durward Eliza C. Downie Wilson Wm. Iddulton	
By Whom Married	22	Revd A. Grant	Revd A. Grant	
License or Banns	23	L.	L.	
Date of Registration	24	September 28, 1906	September 28, 1906	

015923   015924

80

Ontario Marriage

The marriage was registered by the officiating clergyman in Downie Township, Perth County, within two weeks of the event. Religious affiliations and occupations of the couple had been long-time requirements on the registration form. The birth (maiden) surname of the mothers of the bride and groom was also specifically requested. Parents' names as given on a marriage record should be confirmed from additional sources. The groom was a widowed farmer from Mordan [*sic*], Manitoba, which may be a good clue to where to find the couple in the next census return. One of the witnesses resides in Tonawanda, New York, perhaps providing a new direction to explore potential kinship relations.

Thompson–Jickling, Ontario marriage registration 015923 (1906); Archives of Ontario microfilm MS 932 reel 124.

Register of Baptisms &c.
1835.

Names.	
Interment of Michael Carey Died on the 5 Inst. 1.	February the 8th was Interred, in the Catholic Cemetry of Niagara, Michael Carey, aged 36 years, a Native of the county Cavan Ireland. There were present at his funeral: James McGarry, Matthew Donahue William Keating, Hugh McNally & others. By one Edwd. Gordon P.
Profession of Faith made by Martha Hammond 1.	February 9th Martha Hammond, aged 13 years, made a public profession of the Catholic Faith renounced the errors of Protestantism and was in due form received into the Catholic Church. Signd by the Convert. In presence of John Harris, Thomas Harrington Hugh McNally & others. By one E. Gordon P.
Martha Hammond	February 9th Baptized (Sub Con.) Martha Hammond aged 13 years, daughter of John Hammond (deceasd) and Martha Jones. Sponsors: Andrew Boylan and MaryAnne Boylan his wife By one Edwd. Gordon P.
Marriage James Mahoney to Martha Hammond	February 11th was married in the C. Church of Niagara, after one publication of their Banns, James Mahoney and Martha Hammond the former is Son of Bryan Mahoney and Ellen Power Parish of Bannow, C. Wexford Ireland the latter is Daughter of John Hammond (deceased) and Martha Jones, Native of Shropshire England. Hugh McNally, Witnesses Thomas Whitty Daniel McDugal Andrew & Co. By one E. Gordon P.
John Molloy 11.	February 16th Baptized John, aged 2 weeks, son of David Molloy & Catherine Quinn, residing in Niagara Sponsor Margaret Harris. By one E. Gordon P.

Niagara Church Register

This is a photocopy of another original church register page. If the prime goal was finding the marriage of James Mahoney and Martha Hammond, would the researcher read the entire page? Certain observances were undertaken by Martha before the marriage. First she made a public profession of faith, or conversion, for acceptance into the Catholic Church. Her age is stated and more than three witnesses were present. A week later she was baptized with her parents being named and a married couple as official sponsors. Two days following, the marriage took place. It not only gives the names of parents, but also the Mahoney family's native parish in Ireland and the Hammond county of origin in England. Each piece of information must be evaluated for its weight as evidence.

St. Vincent de Paul Catholic Church (Niagara-on-the-Lake, Ontario), "Register of Baptisms, Marriages and Burials, 1827–1846," unpaginated, Martha Hammond (1835); Archives of Ontario microfilm MS 544.

Cemetery Marker

A cemetery stone is an original source because it is the first creation of this form (unless one has evidence that it was a later replacement). However, the information recorded on it is considered secondary because the stone carver was rarely someone with firsthand knowledge of the death. The name and date of death are direct evidence and often accurate. Other information about ages and "native of" may be secondary, but could provide reliable clues to the question of year and place of birth. A bonus in this example is the name of a sister of Patrick, probably her married name.

McCristle stone marker, St. Michael's Cemetery, Toronto, Ontario; photograph by Ruth Chernia, 2003.

Form C.

PROVINCE OF MANITOBA.

OFFICIAL NOTICE OF DEATH.

Particulars to be registered touching a death to be supplied to the Division Registrar

of _____ *Winnipeg* _____ by informant other than
Physician or Coroner before a permit of burial can be issued.

1. Full name of deceased (Initials only not accepted; if an unnamed child, give surname preceded by "unnamed")	Surname	Dougall
	Given name	Peter
2. If married or widowed give full maiden name	Surname	
	Given name	
3. Sex		Male
4. Color or race (white, black (negro or negra descent), Indian, Japanese, Chinese or other)		White
5. Date of death	Month June day 13 19 14	
6. Place of death (street and house number or lot and block number or number of parish or river lot, or fractional section, township and range; if in a hospital, etc., give its name)	234 River Ave	
7. Date of birth	Month Sept day 18 1824	
8. Age	89 Years 8 months 16 days	
9. Place of birth (if in Manitoba, give exact location; if in Canada, province, city, town, village or nearest post office; if foreign, state the country and post office address)	Linlithgow, Scotland	
10. Length of residence at place of death and in Province	At place of death 9 yrs In Province 9 yrs	
11. Occupation (children and adults not engaged at some gainful employment should be marked "None")	Retired	
12. Single, married, widowed or divorced	Married	
13. Full name of father	John Dougall	
14. Birthplace of father (same as Item No. 9)	Scotland	
15. Maiden name of mother	Mary Hastie	
16. Birthplace of mother (same as Item No. 9)	Scotland	
17. Name of physician who attended deceased. (where physician did not attend, state probable cause of death)	Dr Beath	
18. Your relationship to deceased	Son	
19. Were you in the house at the time of death?	Yes	
20. Signature and address of informant	The above-stated particulars are true to the best of my knowledge and belief. Signature of Informant Geo. J. Dougall	
	Address 234 River Ave	
21. Date of Information	June 16th 1914	
22. Registered number filed this 16	1660	June 19 14
		Signature of Division Registrar

REMARKS:

After being filled up, this form is to be sent to the Clerk of the Municipality in which the death occurred. It will be transmitted postage free if the envelope is left unsealed, and has marked on the upper right-hand corner, above the address, the words "Vital Statistics Returns—Free."

PLEASE TURN OVER

Some Illustrated Examples

Manitoba Death

This is an official death document, not a registrar's abstract, signed by the informant. The son George was present at the death, giving primary information about the death event from which we draw direct evidence. Details about age and parents' names represent secondary information, albeit also providing direct evidence of approximate birth year and relationship. Directory searches would confirm whether the place of death was actually the residence of the deceased. The stated place of birth, Linlithgow, was a great clue to "bridging the Atlantic gap," but later investigation showed this was a reference not to the town of that name, but to the former county of Linlithgowshire, which is now West Lothian for record-searching purposes. The true name of Peter's mother was Marion; "Mary" may be a phonetic error on the clerk's part of the form or due to George's pronunciation, indicating that even official sources can have faulty information.

Peter Dougall, Manitoba death registration 1060 (1914); Office of the Division Registrar, Province of Manitoba.

Burials — Niagara 1794 —

January

9 John Butler of Thomas an Infant —
— Young, Wife of John 4 Mile Creek
25 M. Kerr Wife of Robert Kerr Esqr.

March

20 Privt Wyndham of the 5th Regt. shot himself
Corporal Lamb of the 5th Regt.

April

26 Mrs E. Hill Wife of Adjutant Hill

July a child of a poor stranger call'd Chambers

Sepr 9 A soldier surfeited by drinking cold Water

17 — Longwell of the 5th Regt. —

October 7 — Wife of James Chambers

21 James Chambers, an unfortunate stranger.

Novr

11 Anthony Slingerland

Decr

15th Mr Barnham, a stranger: dropt down dead!

Burials Niagara

Early burial records generally exist only for the actual congregation of a church and those interred in the churchyard or denominational burying ground. Farm families frequently set aside a place on their properties to bury their own, whether a clergyman was available to officiate or not. The rector of this church made an effort at identification (surviving parent, spouse, or place of residence), and even cause of death when it was unusual, although occasionally a first name was unknown. Such a register may be the only surviving record of a death, especially if grave markers disappeared or were never erected. Recorded by a man who witnessed the interments, the entries here are *burial* dates, not necessarily the same as the dates these people died. The register provides primary information and direct evidence about burials, with indirect evidence about dates of death.

St. Mark's Anglican Church (Niagara-on-the-Lake, Ontario), "Register of Baptisms, Marriages and Burials, 1792–1849," Book 1, 1792–1815, unpaginated (1794); Archives of Ontario microfilm MS 545 reel 1.

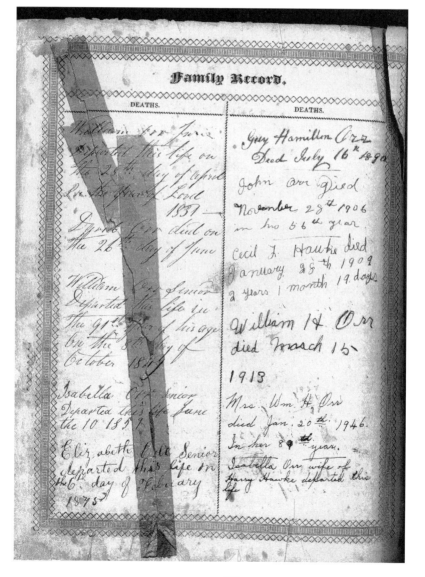

Family Bible Record

A family record in a Bible is an original source and the evidence from which we draw direct evidence, but does it contain primary information? One should check the Bible's publication date to see if it was before or during the time period that is covered. Handwriting differences among the entries suggest that they were made at different times, perhaps soon after the deaths occurred. An exact age at death is helpful, especially if some of these people do not appear on the Bible's page of births. One drawback in many Bible records is that the place of an event and relationships are seldom recorded. Some correlation can be made by examining the pages of births, marriages, and deaths as a whole; constructing a chronological timeline of family events is a useful assessment device.

Hamilton Guy Orr Family Bible Records 1831–1946, *The New Testament of Our Lord and Saviour Jesus Christ* (Cooperstown, NY: H&E Phinney, 1834), "Deaths"; privately held by Orr family, Toronto, Ontario, 2003.

Church. —Constitution.

OBITUARY.

DIED,—In the Township of Clarendon, March 4th, 1843, aged 45, Mrs. MARY McARTHUR, lately the consort of Mr. John McArthur.

The subject of this obituary was born in the United States. Her parents were John and Rebecca Dunlop, who removed to the Township of Chatham, L. C., about 40 years ago. When I travelled the St. Andrew's Circuit I frequently heard that Mrs. Dunlop was a mother in Israel, and had contributed bountifully and cheerfully to the comfort of our early itinerant worthies; and it really seems as if our departed sister had caught the "mantle" of her ascending mother, as in later times the preachers have always had a friend in her—and her house for a home. She was united in marriage to Mr. McArthur in 1817. She was united to Christ by faith in 1829; and, immediately afterwards, united herself to the Methodist Church, of which she continued one of our most consistent members. Thus the instruments of her salvation became the people of her choice; and from the deep piety which her letters breathe, I conclude her faith and religion were scriptural. Her walk through life showed it; and God has shown it upon her surviving children, in having made many of them His children. When I formed an acquaintance with sister McArthur, there was that in her manner and conversation which showed I was associated with more than an ordinary christian. For four years past she was much afflicted with cancer in her throat, which rendered her speech and breathing difficult; and, notwithstanding the aid and skill of six physicians, nature gradually sunk, by protracted illness, till the all-wise God broke the casket to obtain the gem. A few days previous to her death I visited her, and found her sensible, serene, and happy. Her joy was much increased when I informed her of the conversion of her only son. "She turned her face to the wall and wept;" and, like good old Simeon, said, "Lord, now lettest thou thy servant depart in peace, according to thy word; for mine eyes have seen thy salvation." "Her soul was made to magnify the Lord, and her spirit to rejoice in God her Saviour, in thus regarding the lowly estate of his handmaid." I left her in peace; and on my return, in a few days, a mourning family, a vacant chair, and an empty couch, told the 'heavy tidings' that one of my best sisters was gone hence.

"The winter of trouble is past,
The storms of affliction are o'er;
Her struggle is ended at last,
And sorrow and death are no more."

She lived and died a Methodist. An hour previous to her departure, I was informed, she seemed to forget the frailty of nature in the anticipations of glory, and with clear voice sung that heaven-inspired verse,

"Arise, my soul, arise,
Shake off thy guilty fears;
The bleeding Sacrifice
In my behalf appears;
Before the Throne my Surety stands,
My name is written on his hands."

She then requested her daughters to conclude the hymn, and after delivering some advices and instructions to her sorrowing husband, she breathed out her soul saying, "Praise God—praise God—praise God!" Her bereaved husband, children, and friends can truly say, "We sorrow not for her as those without hope." The following was written by her, and deposited among her papers a few days before her death:

"My dear children,—Before you see this I shall have passed through the valley, and joined the redeemed above. While you are weeping, I shall be rejoicing. Yet, if the spirits of the glorified are suffered to visit their earthly friends, I will often come and hover over my dear children, and children's children." Many will say with me, "Let me die her death." WM. DIGNAM.

Newspaper Obituary

Newspapers of the ancestor's locale are a rich source of information, especially obituaries. In newspapers published by religious denominations, tributes to the faithful are often printed, adding so much to a family history. *Christian Guardian* was a Wesleyan Methodist paper. The obituary writer was usually the pastor or a member of the deceased's congregation or, perhaps, a relative who provided the details. Not all are as informative as this one, but most emphasize the Christian virtues of a life well-lived. A person of relatively humble status would rarely rate so much space in a local newspaper. Mary McArthur's life is outlined with her age, place of birth, year of marriage, name of spouse, year of religious conversion, and precise date and place of death. Her parents' names and their residence are included. Along with the description of a death-bed scene, this is wonderful information for a descendant. The information is secondary, but provides direct evidence of events and relationships.

"Obituary," Mary McArthur, *Christian Guardian* (Toronto, Ontario), 10 May 1843, page 115, column 4.

HISTORICAL SKETCH OF

his trials and
, 1904.
here they pros-
gs were uncon-
, and they de-
of Gooderham

cardine, where
he venture was
the *Globe* staff,
for two years,
any.
sided, with the
e machinery of
s.
he Model farm,

us atmosphere
h century, and
mind early in-

mbers of Chal-
, and has since
he is now the

to reside with

uelph *Mercury*,
d his education
cademy. After
Z of the *Wood-*
appointed a re-
. McIntosh was
e late Mr. and

ecretary to the
e death of Mr.
M. Gibson, Hon.
roprietor of the
in 1906, became

d when twelve
when the land
cres, lot 9, con.
e m. Sarah Sin-
race, and when
he Presbyterian
While Mr. Mc-
the respect and
mber since boy-
the homestead

was b. in 1840,
started to earn
e of twenty-one,
, 1865, when he
2, con. 12, for
. 9, con. 12. In
11. About 1880
900, 50 acres of
ether. Mr. Mc-
irst class build-
st piece that he
ted as judge of
nization of the
ar of its opera-
for years. He
ial Fire Ins. Co.
Rothsay Presby-
onservative, and

led his last dol-
this he has by
nest farms with
f its most pros-
alton Co., whose
okkeeper, in To-
c, Jr., at home,
perate the farm

weeks in crossing. His sisters were Mrs. Duncan McArthur, Erin; Mrs. Peter McArthur, Nassagaweya; Mrs. Arch. McLean, Erin, and Mrs. Donald Sinclair, Erin.

His brother John was drowned at Quebec before landing, and Neil still lives in Caledon, on the Erin Tp. line. His mother had a small amount of money, but Donald had only 25c. when he landed in Quebec. After working in Montreal for a short time, and saving a little money, he, in company with his brother-in-law, Duncan McArthur, bought 100 acres, east half lot 5, con. 10, Erin, which they started to clear and put in a crop. After three years Donald purchased his brother-in-law's interest and set there permanently. He finished clearing it, and in 1895 when he retired to Erin Village owned 400 acres of land. He had a fair education, and never took interest in political or municipal affairs. He was Trustee of S.S. No. 1 for about twenty-five years, being always greatly interested in school matters. He kept good stock, and improved his place. Mr. McKechnie was a Presbyterian and a Liberal. He m. Margaret Young, of Erin, who d. 1899, age 73. Issue: Alexander (d.), Jane (d.), Mrs. Gilbert McArthur, Erin; John, Esquesing; James (d. Erin), Daniel (d.), Andrew, Mrs. John Collins, Erin; Margaret, Erin; and Neil, B.C.

Andrew, b. on the homestead in Erin, has always been engaged in farming. He worked at home for years, and for his share of the property received 100 acres, the west half of lot 5, con. 11, Erin, which he sold, and purchased the homestead where he has since resided except for five years, when he rented it and operated his brother's farm on the 8th line. He carries on mixed farming, keeping good grade stock, and takes an active interest in the affairs of the township. He was Trustee of S.S. No. 4 for three years, and at this writing is serving his third term as Township Councillor, being elected the last time by acclamation. In 1894 he m. Mary, dau. of James Marshall, of Brampton. Issue: Mary A. and David.

McKEE, THOMAS (d.), b. Scot. He was a linen weaver by trade, and came to Canada in 1843, and took up land in Wellesley Tp. Issue: Mrs. Thomas Wilson and William.

William, b. in Glasgow, Scot., in 1815, followed his father to Canada in 1844, and worked with him in Wellesley until 1850, when he came to Maryborough Tp. and located 100 acres, the west half of lot 14, con. 3. He took his clearance papers and Crown deed in 1873, and this farm has never passed out of the family. He was a weaver by trade, working at it every fall until his death, at which time there was a piece of cloth in his loom. He was a very industrious and active man, of sterling qualities and a kind disposition. He was a local preacher and a very active worker in the Methodist church, and was instrumental in securing free schools for Maryborough, without which the people of to-day would have had very little educational advantages. In politics he was a Reformer. In 1845 he m. Margaret D. Fleming. He d. in 1882, age 67, while she d. in 1903, age 73. Issue: Mrs. R. King (d.); John, Peterboro'; Mrs. Thos. Faulkner, Maryborough; Thomas, Maryborough; Elizabeth (d.), James, Mary (d.), William (d.), Archibald, Alexander, in B.C.; and David, a missionary in India. James and Archibald were born and raised on the homestead, of which each has 50 acres. They were well read men, good farmers, and are Methodists and Liberals.

McKENZIE, KENNETH (d.), b. 1815; d. 1877, was born in Ross-shire, Scot., and came to Puslinch Tp. in 1843, purchasing a squatter's claim on lot 17, con. 10. After clearing this he increased his holdings to 200 acres by purchasing lot 18, con. 10, and lot 16, con. 11. He was a man of great personal activity, and an extremely hard worker, attending always to his private business, and leaving municipal honors to others who were more eager for them. He was a consistent Presbyterian, and a staunch Liberal. He m. Christina Cameron, who came to Canada in 1832. Issue: Annie, d. in infancy; Archibald, Donald (d. at 26), while studying for the ministry; Annie, at the home farm; Alexander, in Wentworth Co.; Duncan, d. 1900, age 42; Kenneth, Peter, who went to Montana in 1881; Janet, a nurse in Rochester, and Christina at home.

Kenneth, unm., owns and works the homestead, which he has in a first class state of cultivation. He has one of the finest homes in the township, and he and his sisters take pride in keeping it in that condition. Kenneth devotes his entire attention to his farm work, and does not take an active part in municipal or political matters. He makes a specialty of Oxforddown sheep, breeding for the local market. He is a Presbyterian, and a Liberal, and one of the most respected men in the township.

Archibald is a great traveller, having been all over the Western States and Canada several times, as well as to Scotland. He is now in Yorkton, N.W.T. He is a mason by trade, and is unm.

McKERLIE, JOHN, b. Halton Co., was one of the first settlers in Wellington Co. He was a Presbyterian and a Conservative.
John, his son, was b. in Eramosa, 1835, and sat. on the town line

Donald m. Janet Young, and
is a well-known horseman, and h
exhibiting horses.
William m. Annie O'Neil, an
on the old homestead in Erin Tp.
100 acres, and has since added 40
500 acres, upon which is a beaut
carries on mixed farming, and is
cattle, having a herd of fifty hea
with great success. He also ha
among them, two were imported f
is a member of the Disciples churc
held the office of Councillor for on
Commissioner for four years. In 1
of the county of Wellington by
highly respected men in Wellingt
son, in Erin Tp. Issue: Margar
and Ross, at home.

McKNIGHT, GEORGE (d.).
managh, Ire., 1827, where he wa
Smith in Ire., who was also a n
grated to Canada in the early fi
1854 came to Minto, taking up l
roads at this time and the McKni
and up to their location by the
made a small clearing and built
whole farm and living upon it i
him. They were members of the
McKnight was a Conservative. I
Denney, Mrs. Moses Aldridge,
Heckroth. John, m. Elizabeth F
George, m. Mary J. Lovell, and
Samuel, m. Elizabeth Rothwell.
and Clarence. He owns 200 acr
Minto, being an extensive farmer,
ship. Like his father, he is a C
the Church of England.

McLACHLAN, JOHN (d.),
1826, age 35. He was a farmer's
later kept a draper's shop in Stir
set. about one mile from Carleto
Reformer. He m. Ann Houston
borough; Alexander, Caledon; W
Scotland, and James. Finlay Hayes
and James d. Maryborough, b. in
James, b. Carleton Place, d.
trade, and when he came to Mar
east half lot 12, con. 15, there
great many of the houses and b
house is still standing on the pla
for some years, and was active in
of the old Derryadd Church, ala
In politics he was a Reformer.
denced by his working his farm
Sarah J. Ballantyne. of Arthur,
of that township. Issue: Willia
minister, Hanover, Mrs. W. II. (
Brandon; Mrs. Wm. Rinn, Britto
(d. 20); Mrs. Susan Gillrie, Mai
L., Carmen. Man.; Mrs. J. E. (
teacher, Arthur. Mrs. McLachla
Village.

McLAUGHLIN, RICHARD
m. Mary Quigley. They came t
fifty acres of land on the Eramo
Their family were b. on this far
farm and purchased lot 22, con. 4
death in 1853. His sons, John a
and Eramosa, and have since
rented lot 27, con. 4, Eramosa (1
this farm and have since owned

McLEAN, ALEXANDER, b.
the age of 85. He was 16 years
his parents. He cleared the fa
26, a part of which he sold to Pe
ful man, active and aggressive.
always put on the corners in ra
the Presbyterian church, and in
Reeve for three years, and Count

Published Biography

Potted biographies were a feature in many of the late nineteenth-and early twentieth-century Ontario county atlases and, indeed, elsewhere in North America. Information was compiled from residents who usually subscribed to underwrite the cost of publication. Published biographies about pioneers are derivative sources and details about the deceased person often represent secondary information. We treat the information cautiously because we can't necessarily know if the descendant or informant had firsthand knowledge of events in the subject's life. Also, if the subject was alive at the time of publication, primary information could have been provided. Of eight children listed for Kenneth McKenzie, one son and two daughters lived on the homestead farm when the atlas was published. The property references are of great interest, but we see that little vital data are given about their parents. More weight could be attached to information about then-living children, for example, their names and locations, but the facts must be compared with information and evidence culled from a variety of sources.

Historical Atlas of Wellington County, 1906 (1906; reprint Belleville, Ontario: Mika Publishing, 1972), page 46, "Kenneth McKenzie."

five daughters. James, who was councillor for the district at the time of his tragic death in April 1919, married Katie McDonald of Queensville and had issue: five sons and two daughters. Malcolm died in early manhood. David died in British Columbia in 1917, Dan was last heard of in Alaska about twenty-five years ago; Elizabeth died in 1918; Ellen married John McDonald (Butcher) Princeville and had one son and one daughter.

THE McARTHUR'S OF PRINCEVILLE.

John McArthur emigrated from Mull, Scotland, and took up a farm at Princeville. His wife's name was Ann McLachlan. He had a family of three sons, Neil, Alexander and John and two daughters, Janet and Grace.

Neil, married Ann Cameron and had a family of six sons and three daughters, namely: Alexander, Donald, Duncan, James, John and Archy, Mary, Ann and Maggie.

Donald married Annie McIntosh and had issue three sons,: Neil, James and Finlay and four daughters, Mary, Jessie, Margaret and Martha.

Duncan married Mary Jane Cameron and had five sons, John, Neil, Dougald, Abraham and Allan and three daughters: Annie, Margaret and Mary Jane.

Alexander (Neil's son) died in the United States.

James married Flora McDonald and had one son and one daughter.

John Neil's son was drowned at sea.

Archy took up a farm in Manitoba where he still resides.

Mary Neil's daughter married Lauchlin McFadden, River Dennis and had a family of five sons and two daughters.

Ann Neil's daughter married Allan McColl, Glendale, and had issue; five sons and two daughters.

Maggie Neil's daughter married Charles Smith of Gloucester and had a family of three sons and two daughters.

THE McINTOSH'S OF PRINCEVILLE.

John McIntosh emigrated from Glenelg, Scotland with his family about the year 1790 and took up a farm at Princeville where some of his descendants still resides. His wife was Ann McLennan. He had

96

Local History

Local histories are a popular way of recording the history of a community. Similar publication projects extend to histories for churches, businesses, and organizations, among other subjects. Sometimes undertaken by a single compiler, sometimes managed by committee, their content may be a mixture of oral interviews and research in relevant records. In this Cape Breton county, the references to "drowned at sea" and "died in the United States" recur regularly in many families of that region. At least one reference to a drowning was proven erroneous: in reality the man in question had lost touch with his birth family, made his way to Manitoba, and produced a large and healthy family. Note the general lack of dates for events. Again, printed local histories are derivative sources (compilations), with often unattributed secondary information, even though that information may offer direct evidence relevant to our research question. When a surname is common in one area, it is wise to spend time sorting out same-name families that may have been inadvertently mingled by authors.

J.L. McDougall, *History of Inverness County* (1922; reprint Belleville, Ontario: Mika Publishing, 1971), page 247, "The McArthurs of Princeville."

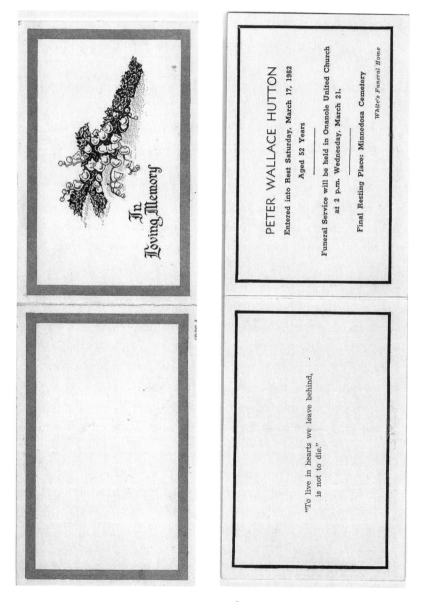

In
Loving Memory

PETER WALLACE HUTTON

Entered into Rest Saturday, March 17, 1962

Aged 52 Years

Funeral Service will be held in Onanole United Church
at 2 p.m. Wednesday, March 21.

Final Resting Place: Minnedosa Cemetery

White's Funeral Home

"To live in hearts we leave behind,
is not to die."

Funeral Card

Many different types of records could have been created at, or soon after, the time of death. Funeral cards, a custom now all but consigned to the past, were a way of communicating death and funeral information to friends in the community. They are original sources with primary information about death, funeral, and burial — direct evidence answering questions of dates and places surrounding a death. Here, the information about the man's age should be secondary, yet it is directly relevant to the issue of his birth year, despite being imprecise. Cards frequently bore a verse of tribute. Nowadays it is becoming common to see cards or programs with a tribute to the deceased distributed at the funeral or memorial service itself.

Peter Wallace Hutton, funeral card announcement, 1962, White's Funeral Home, Minnedosa, Manitoba; privately held by author, Toronto.

Form F.—Certificate of Registration, prepared by the Registrar-General of Ontario.

BURIAL PERMIT.

ALSO

TRANSIT PERMIT.

I Hereby Certify that the particulars of the Death of ...*Mary Autor*... resident in ...*Beaverton*...
(at time of Death.)

caused by ...*apoplexy*...

have been registered by me, and that the provisions of Sections 22, 23 and 25, Chapter 17, Vict. 59, 1896, have been duly complied with.

Signed. ...*C. S. Stinson*...

...........................Division Registrar.

Date Issued ...*July 15*... 180*7*

Municipality of ...*Beaverton*...

Cap. 17, Vict. 59, 1896, Sec. 27. Any person who knowingly or wilfully makes, or causes to be made, a false statement touching any of the particulars required to be reported and entered under this Act, shall upon conviction forfeit the sum of $50.00.

NOTICE—The above words "Transit Permit" must be scored out by the Division Registrar (thus: ~~TRANSIT PERMIT~~, in the case of a death due to anthrax, smallpox, cholera, scarlatina, diphtheria or croup, all which demand, under the Public Health Act, Cap. 205, R.S.O. 1887, private burial in a cemetery in common use by the municipality wherein the death occurred.

Burial Permit

In the late nineteenth century, a burial or transit permit became mandatory before a funeral home could transport a body to a cemetery (note the requirement stated under the heading of the Manitoba Death example). Little information is given on it, but it has name-date-place identification. Neither the funeral home nor the cemetery are mentioned on this paper. If this was the first clue found about Mary Sutor's death, we must not assume the date on the permit is either the date of death or the date of burial. The permit does provide direct evidence of the facts stated thereon.

Mary Sutor, Burial Permit, 1897, Beaverton, Ontario, issued by Registrar General of Ontario; photocopy held by author, Toronto.

Funeral Directors Statement of Death

We certify that _Jane Graham Livingston Merriman_ .... died at

__Guelph, Ontario__ .... on the __15th__ day of __May__ 19 __90__

The funeral of the above named deceased person was conducted by this Funeral Home on

the __20th__ .... day of __May__ .... 19 __90__

with __cremation__ .... at _Woodlawn Crematorium, Guelph, Ontario._

Our records show the next-of-kin to be:

NAME: H. Gordon Merriman

ADDRESS: R.R.#1 Puslinch, Ontario NOB 2JO

RELATIONSHIP: spouse

We certify the above to be a true statement from our records. _Wall-Custance Funeral Home & Chapel_

Dated in __Guelph, Ontario__ .... Prov. _____ 206 Norfolk Street

.... City .... GUELPH -- ONTARIO

this __20th__ .... day of __May__ .... 19 __90__ Per _[signature]_

Funeral Directors' Statement

Another modern requirement, which may vary from one province or state to another, is the issuance of this signed and sealed statement — an original source with primary information and direct evidence of date and place of death. This document is a certificate with legal authority as proof of death although it has fewer details than a government-issued death certificate. Even with a spouse or next of kin providing the information, we must be aware that a primary fact coming from a grieving family could be erroneous. In reality, Jane did not die in the city of Guelph; she died in nearby Puslinch Township. Obviously we would seek other sources and information for comparable evidence. The place of cremation does not necessarily imply that interment of the ashes was made at the same place.

Jane Graham Livingston Hutton, Funeral Directors Statement of Death, 1990, Wall-Custance Funeral Home & Chapel, Guelph, Ontario; privately held by author, Toronto.

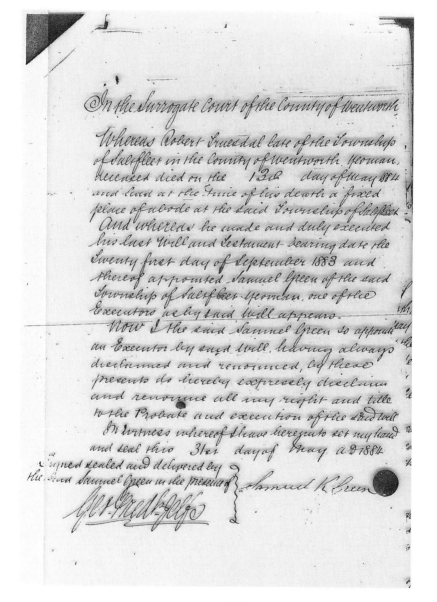

In the Surrogate Court of the County of Wentworth

Whereas Robert Truesdal late of the Township of Saltfleet in the County of Wentworth, Yeoman, deceased died on the 13th day of May 1884 and had at the time of his death a fixed place of abode at the said Township of Saltfleet. And whereas he made and duly executed his last Will and Testament bearing date the Twenty first day of September 1883 and thereof appointed Samuel Green of the said Township of Saltfleet Yeoman, one of the Executors as by said Will appears.

Now I the said Samuel Green so appointed an Executor by said Will, having always disclaimed and renounced, by these presents do hereby expressly disclaim and renounce all my right and title to the Probate and execution of the said Will

In Witness whereof I have hereunto set my hand and seal this 31st day of May AD 1884

Signed sealed and delivered by the said Samuel Green in the presence of

Samuel K. Green

Petition for Probate

An estate file normally contains at least one legal document that states the date and place of death of the testator. If a death registration is not available, this fills a gap in an individual's vital information. The petition made by an executor or would-be administrator to a court for probate is an original source. Thus the information provides direct evidence concerning the decedent's name, death date, and death place. Is that evidence coming from primary information? We may not be able to answer that, unless we know the petitioner is someone who was present when death occurred. Mistakes in date or place do occur, as in the Funeral Directors' Statement. One thing to watch for in evaluating this and other information in an estate file is how much time elapsed between the date of death and the petition.

Robert Truesdal, estate file 2012 (1884), Wentworth County Surrogate Court, R G22-205; Archives of Ontario microfilm GS1-610.

		FOURTH CENSUS OF CANADA, 1901								SCHEDULE TABLEAU No. 1. POPU

A census schedule (Schedule No. 1 — Population) of the Fourth Census of Canada, 1901, Province Ont., District No. 5? North East, showing handwritten entries.

1901 Census Canada

Twentieth-century census returns have much more information than previous enumerations. A census sheet is an original source where the reliability of the information depends on the accuracy of the knowledge of the person who provided it and the accuracy of the enumerator in recording what he was told. Therefore, the information could be a mixture of primary and secondary. Some twentieth-century census returns ask for month, year, and place of birth, or sometimes full birth date. Additionally, these more modern returns may show citizenship details including years of immigration and naturalization if applicable, occupation and employment data, and literacy/language levels. Religion and racial or tribal origin were part of the Canadian questionnaire. But again, much of the information here needs investigation in more sources before credible conclusions can be reached. For instance, many researchers find birth information in a census conflicts with that in other sources.

1901 Census Ontario, district 59, North Essex, sub-district G, Sandwich West, subdivision 1, page 3; Library and Archives Canada microfilm T-6466.

READING AND REFERENCE LIST

Books

Board for Certification of Genealogists. *The BCG Genealogical Standards Manual.* Orem, UT: Ancestry Inc., 2000.

Canada. Department of the Secretary of State. *The Canadian Style: A Guide to Writing and Editing.* Revised edition. Toronto, ON: Dundurn Press, 1997.

The Chicago Manual of Style. Fifteenth edition. Chicago, IL: University of Chicago Press, 2003.

Carmack, Sharon. *You Can Write Your Family History.* 2003. Reprint, Baltimore, MD: Genealogical Publishing Company, 2008.

Christensen, Penelope. *How Do I Prove It?* Third edition. Toronto, ON: Heritage Productions, 2008.

Curran, Joan Ferris, Madilyn Coen Crane, and John H. Wray. *Numbering Your Genealogy: Basic Systems, Complex Families and International Kin.* Revised edition. Arlington, VA: National Genealogical Society, 2008.

Drake, Michael, and Ruth Finnegan, editors, with Jacqueline Eustace. *Studying Family and Community History*, Vol. 4: *Sources and Methods: A Handbook.* UK: Cambridge University Press, 1994.

Fitzpatrick, Colleen. *Forensic Genealogy*. Fountain Valley, CA: Rice Book Press, 2005.

Greenwood, Val D. *The Researcher's Guide to American Genealogy*. Third edition. Baltimore, MD: Genealogical Publishing Company, 2000.

Hatcher, Patricia Law. *Producing a Quality Family History*. Salt Lake City: Ancestry Inc., 1996.

Hoff, Henry B., and Michael J. Leclerc, editors. *Genealogical Writing in the 21st Century: A Guide to Register Style and More*. Second edition. Rockland, ME: Picton Press, 2006.

Jacobus, Donald Lines. *Genealogy as Pastime and Profession*. Second edition revised. Baltimore, MD: Genealogical Publishing Company, 1968.

Mills, Elizabeth Shown. *Evidence! Citation and Analysis for the Family Historian*. Baltimore, MD: Genealogical Publishing Company, 1997.

———. *Evidence Analysis: A Research Process Map*. Washington, DC: Board for Certification of Genealogists, 2006.

———. *Evidence Explained: Citing Historical Sources from Artifacts to Cyberspace*. Second edition. Baltimore, MD: Genealogical Publishing Company, 2009.

———. *QuickSheet: Citing Ancestry.com® Databases and Images, Evidence! Style*. Baltimore, MD: Genealogical Publishing Company, 2009.

———. *QuickSheet: Citing Online Historical Sources, Evidence! Style*. First revised edition. Baltimore, MD: Genealogical Publishing Company, 2007.

Mills, Elizabeth Shown, editor. *Professional Genealogy: A Manual for Researchers, Writers, Editors, Lecturers and Librarians*. Baltimore, MD: Genealogical Publishing Company, 2001.

Rose, Christine. *Genealogical Proof Standard: Building a Solid Case*. fourth edition. San Jose, CA: Rose Family Association, 2009.

Rubincam, Milton. *Pitfalls in Genealogical Research*. Salt Lake City, UT: Ancestry, 1987.

Stevenson, Noel C. *Genealogical Evidence: A Guide to the Standard of Proof Relating to Pedigrees, Ancestry, Heirship and Family History*. Revised edition. Laguna Hills, CA: Aegean Park Press, 1989.

Internet

Quotation marks (" ") indicate specific links on the website.

Ancestry.com and *Ancestry.ca*. "Learning Center." *www.ancestry.com*.

Association of Professional Genealogists. *www.apgen.org*. Mail list: *APGPublicList-request@apgen.org*.

Board for Certification of Genealogists. "Genealogy's Standards," "Skillbuilding: Your Learning Center." *www.bcgcertification.org*.

Eastman, Dick. Eastman's Online Genealogy Newsletter. Articles in Plus Edition, Podcasts, and Videos. *blog.eogn.com*.

Family History Library. "Research Helps." *www.familysearch.org*.

Gormley, Myra Vanderpool. "Genealogical Frauds: Traps for the Imprudent." RootsWeb Freepages. *freepages.genealogy.rootsweb. ancestry.com/~tmark/GeneFraudsArticle.html*.

Hare, Alison. "Citations for Canadians." Ontario Chapter of the Association of Professional Genealogists. *ocapg.org*.

International Commission for Accreditation of Professional Genealogists (ICAPGen). "Consumer Information." *www.icapgen.org*.

International Society of Family History Writers and Editors. "Columns" newsletter. *isfhwe.org*. Mail list: *ISFHWE-L@ rootsweb.com*.

National Genealogical Society. "References for Researching," "Tutorials," "NGS Standards and Guidelines," "Publications," "*NGS Quarterly*," "Editorial Process." *www.ngsgenealogy.org*.

New England Historic Genealogical Society. "Programs and Events," "Online Seminars," "Publications," "The Register," "Submitting an Article." *www.newenglandancestors.org.*

Articles

Only a few samples can be shown here from the many journals and magazines available.

Camp, Anthony B. "Fraud and Deception in Genealogy." *Families* (Ontario Genealogical Society). Vol. 34 (February 1995): 15–25.

Devine, Donn. "Sorting Relationships Among Families with the Same Surname: An Irish-American DNA Study." *National Genealogical Society Quarterly.* Vol. 93 (2005): 283–93.

Forsythe, Warren L. "Resolving Conflicts Between Records: A Spurious Moseley Family Bible." *National Genealogical Society Quarterly.* Vol. 84 (September 1996):182–99.

Hare, Alison. "Citations for Canadians." *Families.* Vol. 42 (2003):165–67.

Hill, Ronald A. "Using Records to Understand Ancestral Motives: The Thwarted Will of Christopher Lean of Cornwall." *National Genealogical Society Quarterly.* Vol. 92 (2004): 269–84.

Holsclaw, Birdie Monk. "From Hypothesis to Proof: Indirect Evidence for the Maiden Identity of Elizabeth, wife of George Hagenburger." *National Genealogical Society Quarterly.* Vol. 92 (2004): 96–104.

Jones, Thomas W. "A Conceptual Model of Genealogical Evidence: Linkage between Present-Day Sources and Past Facts." *National Genealogical Society Quarterly.* Vol. 86 (March 1998): 5–18.

Jones, Thomas W. "Organizing Meager Evidence to Reveal Lineages — An Irish Example: Geddes of Tyrone." *National Genealogical Society Quarterly.* Vol. 89 (2001): 98–112.

Leary, Helen F.M. "Evidence Revisited — DNA, POE, and GPS." *OnBoard* (Newsletter of the Board for Certification of Genealogists). Vol. 4 (January 1998): 1–2, 5.

Leary, Helen F.M. "Sally Hemings' Children: A Genealogical Analysis of the Evidence." *National Genealogical Society Quarterly.* Vol. 89 (September 2001): 165–207.

Mathews, Barbara J. "Structural Elements of a Good Genealogy." *OnBoard.* Vol. 11 (January 2006): 1–2.

Mills, Elizabeth Shown. "Genealogy in the 'Information Age': History's New Frontier?" *National Genealogical Society Quarterly.* Vol. 91 (December 2003): 260–77.

Mills, Elizabeth Shown and Gary B. "The Genealogist's Assessment of Alex Haley's *Roots.*" *National Genealogical Society Quarterly.* Vol. 72 (March 1984): 35–49.

National Genealogical Society Quarterly (selected) Special Issues: *Evidence.* Vol. 87 (September 1999); *Putting Family History into Context.* Vol. 88 (December 2000); *Genealogy and Genetics.* Vol. 93 (December 2005); *Law and Genealogy.* Vol. 95 (September 2007).

Rising, Marsha Hoffman. "Examining and Analyzing the Family Bible." *National Genealogical Society Quarterly.* Vol. 90 (December 2002): 257–69.

NOTES

1. Anthony J. Camp, "Forgery and Deception in Genealogy," *Families* (Ontario Genealogical Society), Vol. 34 (February 1995): 15–25.

2. Gary B. Mills and Elizabeth S. Mills, "Roots and the New 'Faction': A Legitimate Tool for Clio?" *The Virginia Magazine of History and Biography*, Vol. 89 (January 1981): 3–26.

3. Helen Hinchliff, "Caveat Emptor: Family Values," *NGS Newsletter*, Vol. 21 (May–June 1995): 62.

4. Milton Rubincam, "Introduction," *Genealogy as Pastime and Profession*, Donald Lines Jacobus, revised second edition (Baltimore, MD: Genealogical Publishing Company, 1968).

5. Elizabeth Shown Mills, *Evidence Explained: Citing History Sources from Artifacts to Cyberspace* (Baltimore, MD: Genealogical Publishing Company, Inc., 2007), 16.

6. *The BCG Genealogical Standards Manual* (Orem, UT: Ancestry Publishing, 2000), 1–2.

7. Donn Devine, "Evidence Analysis," *Professional Genealogy: A Manual for Researchers, Writers, Editors, Lecturers and Librarians* (Baltimore, MD: Genealogical Publishing Company, 2001), 340.

8. Elizabeth Shown Mills, *Evidence Explained: Citing History Sources from Artifacts to Cyberspace* (Baltimore, MD: Genealogical Publishing Company, 2007), 38.

9. The Canadian Heraldic Authority (Ottawa: Office of the Governor General, 1990), 16.

10. The addresses here may be for societies because editorial addresses change from time to time.

OTHER GENEALOGIST'S
REFERENCE SHELF TITLES

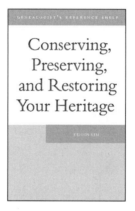

CONSERVING, PRESERVING,
AND RESTORING YOUR HERITAGE
A Professional's Advice
Kennis Kim
978-1-55488-462-9 $19.99

Our family history may be held in documents, photographs, books, clothing, or textiles; sometimes complete collections of items such as coins, trading cards, or stamps. As custodians of pieces of our history, we are faced with how to maintain these items. Here's all you need to determine what you can do yourself to preserve your precious things for future generations.

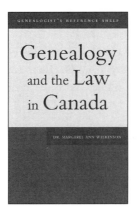

GENEALOGY AND THE LAW IN CANADA
Dr. Margaret Ann Wilkinson
978-1-55488-452-0 $19.99

The development of digital records and broad access to the web has revolutionized the ways in which genealogists approach their investigations — and has made it much easier to locate relevant information. The law, on the other hand, remains very connected to particular geographic locations. This book discusses the relevant laws — access to information, protection of personal data, and copyright — applicable to those working within Canada with materials that are located in Canada.

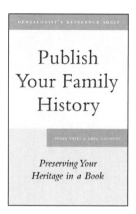

PUBLISH YOUR FAMILY HISTORY
Preserving Your Heritage in a Book
Susan Yates and Greg Ioannou
978-1-55488-727-9 $19.99

Many people want to write a family history, but few ever take on the job of publishing one. *Publish Your Family History* will tell you all the fundamentals of book production, together with the important details that distinguish a home-published book from a homemade one.

Available at your favourite bookseller.

DUNDURN
www.dundurn.com